Markets, Power, and Change

Stefan Fröhlich

Markets, Power, and Change

Germany's Geoeconomic Turning Point

Stefan Fröhlich
Institut für Politische Wissenschaft
Universitat Erlangen-Nürnberg
Erlangen, Bayern, Germany

ISBN 978-3-658-47048-7   ISBN 978-3-658-47049-4 (eBook)
https://doi.org/10.1007/978-3-658-47049-4

Translation from the German language edition: "Märkte, Macht und Wandel" by Stefan Fröhlich, © Der/die Herausgeber bzw. der/die Autor(en), exklusiv lizenziert an Springer Fachmedien Wiesbaden GmbH, ein Teil von Springer Nature 2024. Published by Springer Fachmedien Wiesbaden. All Rights Reserved.

This book is a translation of the original German edition "Märkte, Macht und Wandel" by Stefan Fröhlich, published by Springer Fachmedien Wiesbaden GmbH in 2024. The translation was done with the help of an artificial intelligence machine translation tool. A subsequent human revision was done primarily in terms of content, so that the book will read stylistically differently from a conventional translation. Springer Nature works continuously to further the development of tools for the production of books and on the related technologies to support the authors.

© The Editor(s) (if applicable) and The Author(s), under exclusive license to Springer Fachmedien Wiesbaden GmbH, part of Springer Nature 2025

This work is subject to copyright. All rights are solely and exclusively licensed by the Publisher, whether the whole or part of the material is concerned, specifically the rights of translation, reprinting, reuse of illustrations, recitation, broadcasting, reproduction on microfilms or in any other physical way, and transmission or information storage and retrieval, electronic adaptation, computer software, or by similar or dissimilar methodology now known or hereafter developed.

The use of general descriptive names, registered names, trademarks, service marks, etc. in this publication does not imply, even in the absence of a specific statement, that such names are exempt from the relevant protective laws and regulations and therefore free for general use.

The publisher, the authors and the editors are safe to assume that the advice and information in this book are believed to be true and accurate at the date of publication. Neither the publisher nor the authors or the editors give a warranty, expressed or implied, with respect to the material contained herein or for any errors or omissions that may have been made. The publisher remains neutral with regard to jurisdictional claims in published maps and institutional affiliations.

Cover picture: © Schab, Adobe Stock, 244617706

This Springer imprint is published by the registered company Springer Fachmedien Wiesbaden GmbH, part of Springer Nature.
The registered company address is: Abraham-Lincoln-Str. 46, 65189 Wiesbaden, Germany

If disposing of this product, please recycle the paper.

Contents

1 **Why this Book—Instead of a Foreword**   1
References   14

2 **The Global Turning Point has Long Since Occurred**   15
Europe's Late Awakening   16
The End of German Illusions   18
References   23

3 **The Beginning of the Post-American Era**   25
The Return of Great Power Politics   26
  On the Future of Globalization   33
  The System Competition and the Change in the Global Balance of Power   37
References   42

4 **The Geoeconomic Maps of the Future**   45
The Importance of Geoeconomics   46

The American-Chinese Trade War	51
The Shift of World Trade Towards the Global South	66
In the Shadow of the Superpowers—Europe's Dilemmas	72
From the "Brussels Effect" to "de-risking"	80
"Global Gateway", Transatlantic Trade and the Search for Strategic Partners	93
References	102

5 Germany's Previous Economic Model Under Scrutiny — 107

Between Technology Security, Diversification, and Connectivity	114
A New China Strategy	121
Europe as a lever, the US as an ally	125
References	139

6 The End of Western Complacency — 141

Reference	150

1

Why this Book—Instead of a Foreword

Crises are great accelerators. They bring to light things that have long been kept hidden. The Russian attack on Ukraine in February 2022 has brought many certainties, which were considered irrefutable for Germany and Europe since the fall of the Berlin Wall, to collapse. Since reunification, politicians and academics and journalists belonging to the liberal mainstream have deluded the German public with the illusion of a world in which "change through trade," "cooperative security," "critical dialogue with all," and "renunciation of violence instead of credible deterrence" promised the containment of all conflicts and peaceful coexistence. All visions of a liberal order, in which, following the Kantian logic, free trade and open markets had a peace-building and democracy-promoting effect, could not, however, disguise the fact that the new political reality, viewed from a contemporary historical perspective, was different only a short time later. The hope that the world would democratize did not last long. After the last wave of democratization in the early 1990s, the pendulum soon swung back towards autocratization, particularly in the so-called Global South. According to a study by Freedom House, by 2023 only 5% of people in Asia and 7% of people in Africa lived in free democracies (Freedom House 2023). Failing states, ethnic conflicts, new security risks (international terrorism, climate change, pandemics), multinational corporations and financial service providers that eluded state control, left a feeling of insecurity and loss of control by state institutions among citizens in Europe and the US over the last one and a half decades—with the long-term consequences of the increase in populist movements and tendencies towards autocratization in countries like Poland, Hungary or Italy. Thus, the search for like-minded people is becoming more difficult for the West.

Looking at the global developments of the 21st century, the resulting failures of the past two decades become all too clear: the misjudgment of Russia's development, the energy dependence on its raw materials, the illusion of being able to afford its own China policy in contrast to the United States. Carried by the euphoria that accompanied the implosion of the Soviet Union in the West, especially in Germany, people paid homage to the culture of military restraint and an economic model that, while earning the country the title of export world champion for years, exposed it abroad to accusations of being a security policy and economic free rider.

In retrospect, it is astonishing how persistently the continent and the country, despite many warning voices, long refused to face the realities of an increasingly "out of joint world" (Frank Walter Steinmeier). It has been clear since the global financial crisis of 2007/8 at the latest that the rules of international organizations such as the United Nations, the International Monetary Fund (IMF) or the

World Trade Organization (WTO) cannot contain geopolitical power claims, nationalisms and revisionist thinking in terms of large spaces and are increasingly reaching their limits. Neither do the states that have benefited most from the opening of markets since 1989 (China in particular) accept the basic principles of the liberal order, nor do they adhere to the few rules known to international law, or are they really interested in their global dissemination. Instead, they reduce the market under the primacy of politics to the greatest possible efficiency, assert their own order claims in their "spheres of influence", found alternative formats to the international institutions still dominated by the West (including BRICS, Shanghai Cooperation Organization (SCO) and at best develop a tactical-instrumental understanding of collective security systems like the United Nations. The German turning point proclaimed by the Chancellor in February 2022, it must be stated, is thus once again a belated one in a global turning point that has long been taking place.

This is determined by **three major trends** that overlap and mutually reinforce each other and will prevent the formation of a stable global order in the long run: the return of geopolitics already proclaimed during the Ukraine conflict in 2014 in the wake of the imperial power claims mainly by Russia and China (Taiwan); the struggle of states for global supply chains, secure energy supply, critical raw materials and foreign economic dependencies; and finally, the associated system competition between democracies on the one hand and autocracies (especially China and Russia) on the other, often stylized by politicians and scientists as the end of a three-decade hegemonic global order, also described as "Pax Americana". They will be presented and explained in the **first part of the book**.

In the author's view, it is an irony of history that this development was the result of globalization, and that this in turn only worked because the US, as a hegemon interested in it, together with the Europeans, determined its rules and guaranteed its functioning. The economic historian Charles Kindleberger and the US sociologist Albert Hirschmann coined the term "benevolent hegemon" for this connection between political and economic order as early as the 1970s, who, thanks to his military, political and economic power, provides a liberal world economic order from which ideally everyone benefits. Such a world will not exist again so quickly, and on closer inspection it has never really existed. The liberal order was never a global one, but one dominated by the Western world, which practically excluded the rest of the world. Only for a brief moment in history, namely in the first decade after the collapse of the Soviet Union, was there hope that this order would become a global one. It broke down not least because of Western ideas of humanitarian intervention and regime change. But neither will the Pax Americana be replaced by a Pax Sinica; globalization and worldwide economic interdependencies should ensure this. The world has become too complicated, the sequence has become a simultaneous rivalry of states and no longer allows a new hegemonic order.

The main part is dedicated to the central theme of the volume—the geo-economic power struggle at a global level and its consequences for Europe and German foreign and foreign economic policy. The starting point of the considerations is the thesis, certainly unpopular against the background of the war in Ukraine for many observers, that this, despite all its cruelty and catalytic effect on German foreign policy, represents a singular event, but does not pose an existential threat to the country—provided it finally makes its overdue security policy contribution to credible deterrence in Europe. An attack on NATO territory or Germany seems unlikely in this case. Rather, the war is likely to lead to a "frozen conflict" for the foreseeable future, or even a division of Ukraine in a worst-case scenario, leading to a readjustment of German foreign and security policy without Russia, which, however, poses a solvable task for the country and Europe provided they finally develop credible deterrence forces even without the US.

The actual, much larger strategic challenge for Europe and Germany, in the author's view, is the increasingly rough geo-economic power struggle between the major powers US, China and the EU for technological leadership, raw materials, water and energy. It can indeed become an existential threat and the well-being of Europe and Germany depends on its outcome. The geopolitical change of times must therefore be followed by the geo-economic change of times. This will be the actual generational task for Germany.

In the first chapter of the main part, the term "geo-economics" is first briefly explained and historically classified. The trend towards more protectionism, embargoes and sanctions up to economic wars has always been a basic component of international politics. Only after the end of the Cold War did it enter the academic debate under the term "geo-economics". At that time, the American military strategist Edward N. Luttwak described this caesura as a turning point that relativized the importance of military means for exercising power in international relations in favor of the targeted use of economic instruments. In practice, however, the liberalization of financial and capital markets that began at the end of the 1980s and the integration of emerging and developing countries into the global markets initially promised more growth and prosperity for all. What since then for almost two decades actually brought the world consistently higher growth rates of trade and helped to lift a large part of humanity out of the greatest poverty, did not prevent the increase in inequality worldwide and left globalization losers in all societies. Above all, the global financial crisis of 2008/2009 made it palpable in the West that trade and networking also create more dependence and vulnerability, which can also be used to exert economic pressure.

Since then, geo-economic tensions have increased and threaten to increasingly escalate into a global trade war, with devastating consequences for the world economy. What began from the perspective of the West with Trump and Brexit, continues under Biden's "buy American" policy and China's increased isolation policy and reached its provisional climax with the Corona pandemic, the war in Ukraine and the re-election of Trump in 2024. Worldwide, protectionism and the use of economic instruments for power-political purposes are on the rise. States resort to targeted sanctions in trade with goods, services and dual-use goods, impose entry and export restrictions or block access to bonds, financial transactions or economic aid. They review their supply of food, medical products, energy, critical raw materials and technology. Russia and India already restricted their grain exports before the war in Ukraine, thereby exacerbating price volatility in agricultural products, Vietnam did the same with rice. At the same time, others (Egypt and Tunisia) began to fill the gap in the markets, thereby keeping their own economy afloat. Such developments increasingly compensate for the missing (power) means of multilateral institutions such as the UN, the IMF or the WTO in dealing with global supply crises in the regions most affected.

In the second step, the dramatic deterioration of the American-Chinese relationship as a driver for the worldwide increase in geo-economic power struggles is first analyzed, before the role of the EU in this power struggle is discussed.

1 Why this Book—Instead of a Foreword

The starting point in the global geo-economic power struggle is the rivalry between the two superpowers, the US and China; they are the main drivers of this development, in the shadow of which emerging countries, but also Europe as a whole, have become more protectionist. During the pandemic alone, the number of newly introduced protectionist measures worldwide has increased by almost 25%—a trend that is certainly being reinforced by the war in Ukraine.

In the US, many blame China for its aggressive foreign economic policy. Indeed, complaints about unfair Chinese practices led to Washington regularly summoning China to the WTO dispute settlement panel and imposing initial punitive tariffs, even under the Obama administration. It is obvious that such accusations also involve fear of losing one's own leadership role. Since then, Washington has viewed China's economic and military modernization as the greatest security policy challenge for the country, across party lines. Meanwhile, the American and Chinese economies are of a similar magnitude, although the American one is still significantly larger at given exchange rates of the currencies. However, given the strong growth rates of the Chinese economy over the last three decades, any extrapolation appears threatening to Washington.

The strategic rivalry between the US and China is increasingly solidifying into a permanent global conflict constellation, which in the worst case could also result in a limited military confrontation between the two superpowers in the Pacific, which would have more dramatic consequences for the world economy than the war in Ukraine. Should China attack Taiwan, Europe and Germany can abandon their ambitious plans towards climate neutrality. Although the lights will not go out overnight, as some pessimists even believe, raw materials, iron and steel, as well as laptops and smartphones will be missing in key sectors, and it is doubtful whether sanctions would have any effect in such a case, let alone whether they would be possible at all.

At the same time, the geo-economic power struggle between the two heavyweights promotes a stronger concentration of international trade and harms cooperation. Even though this trend has been noticeable since 2008, current discussions about greater diversification of supply chains and greater autarky show that it has intensified with the pandemic and the war in Ukraine. While the majority of world trade still takes place on global markets, about 40% of it is handled in markets with a high concentration, where countries rely on just two or three suppliers (McKinsey Global Institute 2022).

This brings us to a central development for the world economy. The use of economic instruments for (geo) political purposes has not brought an end to globalization, at most the process has slowed down. What is striking, though little noticed, is the increasing concentration or stronger regionalization of trade flows around the three power centers of the world economy: for the US, the Americas, for China the Asia-Pacific region, and for the EU, trade among member states each have by far the largest share of their foreign trade. Most academics, practitioners, and citizens interested in internal politics are blinded by the media fixation on mutual dependencies and the importance of the three major trade giants US, China, and Europe for the world economy—hence their concern about confronting Beijing. They overlook the fact that the volume of US trade with Canada and Mexico, with a share of more than 30% of total US exports, is four times higher than that with China (2021, 8.6%). Even in terms of imports, China, as the US most important import country with a share of 18.5%, does not come close to the volume of trade with Canada and Mexico. A similar picture emerges for China, whose trade shares in the Asia-Pacific region (Hong Kong, Japan, South Korea, and Taiwan) are now more than twice as large as those with the US (12.5%). Taiwan alone has a similar trade volume with China as with Germany (each around 4%). And for the EU, while a third of trade is with the US and China, trade within the EU clearly predominates at the member state level. For Germany alone, the share of exports to the EU has consistently accounted for more than 50% of total German export volume for years.

This trend has been reinforced at least since Covid by increasing calls for boycotts against foreign countries at the national level worldwide. Once again, the economy is anticipating a development that politics is following much too slowly. Long ago, globally active companies here too began to shorten global supply chains ("near-shoring") and to relocate production to "trustworthy" countries ("friend-shoring") or even to bring it "home" ("reshoring"). Even before the outbreak of the war in Ukraine, about 10% of German companies stated in a survey that they intend to source more intermediate products and materials from their home or EU area in the future, thus shortening their supply chains (Flach et al. 2021).

For a long time trailing behind development and exposed to criticism from expert circles that Europe is missing the connection and is at risk of falling by the wayside in the geo-economic power struggle between the US and China, the EU Commission is now also pursuing a more aggressive foreign economic policy, which also puts pressure on Germany. After European and German companies achieved record sales in the Chinese market for decades, but are now losing market shares, not least because of China's isolationist policy, it is becoming increasingly clear to many in Brussels; Beijing has been making no secret of its plans for world domination for years. The goal in Brussels is now to reduce the risk of too great a dependency ("de-risking") without completely decoupling from China. A series of proposals from the past two years shows that Brussels is willing to use its own geo-economic potential more strongly and to advance from being a pawn to an actor in this power struggle.

In the third chapter of the main part, the author turns to the question of how Germany must deal with these challenges. As a country that, like hardly any other worldwide, is dependent on international trade and therefore insists on adherence to the principles of openness and sustainability, Germany, according to the prevailing opinion among economists and politicians, cannot afford to decouple from the global sales markets. This may be true in principle, but it does not mean that there is no way out of dependencies on China and other system changers; even in the case of Russia, hardly anyone in this country could have imagined this until a year ago. And certainly, such a knockout argument cannot mean to simply continue as before and to conduct foreign economic policy primarily under commercial aspects.

Yes, it is true, Germany is more deeply integrated into global economic chains than most other major industrial nations. 60% of our value creation, as calculated by the Ifo Institute, depends on demand from abroad, and the import of preliminary products plays an equally important role for our competitiveness. Against this background, globalization cannot be easily reversed. Nevertheless, the argument of a threatening collapse of the German GDP by 10% is no more convincing than the warning that a withdrawal from international production networks does not necessarily mean less susceptible production processes at home.

With the exception of some Republicans in the US, no one is talking about an economic decoupling or

1 Why this Book—Instead of a Foreword

Europeanization of supply chains in this form. It is rather about mitigating the disastrous trend towards a concentration of dependencies by identifying and specifically reducing them. German companies have been doing this for several years. The same "either, or" argument is unfortunately also heard from some economists and politicians in connection with the EU Commission's plans for a stronger European industrial policy. They warn against such political planning and refer to the textbook platitude that companies achieve their comparative cost advantages through the market. Does this mean that we simply ignore the geopolitical conflicts and the risks associated with them for us in the hope that somehow the Chinese sales market will remain open to us? What does Beijing's "Made in China 2025" initiative mean other than the intention of greater independence from the West, when Chinese producers should be able to produce 70% of "core competencies and materials" themselves in the future? What happens when the "peace dividend", which Germany apparently thought it could live off forever, becomes the "war dividend" of the autocracies? It is astonishing how in a country whose economic model is known to be against monopolies, some apparently find it hardly worth mentioning that the political leadership in China, for example, just secured state access to more than 60% of rare earths in January 2022, immediately before the outbreak of war in Ukraine.

Against this background, Germany must adapt to the geo-economic challenges and pursue a more active and geographically broader trade and economic policy. It must *firstly* prevent the further transfer of technical knowledge to *domestic* companies in autocratic systems, where these do not adhere to the rules of the global trade regime, associated with exports and direct investments. This is actually also in the company's interest, but should at least not be facilitated by investment and export credit guarantees for individual companies and entire sectors, Hermes guarantees for foreign projects or even rescue by the taxpayer on the part of politics.

Secondly, domestic investments in cutting-edge technologies and critical infrastructure must be facilitated and at the same time the settlement of undesirable investors in Germany must be prevented, where these, as in the case of Huawei's advance into critical telephone infrastructure, affect the country's security policy interests. One does not have to follow the French logic in detail, but Germany also cannot avoid a more active industrial policy. It should be remembered that even the dominant economy in the world, the US, in the past despite rhetoric to the contrary from the lean state, always conducted classic industrial policy by awarding research and development contracts from the Pentagon and buying almost the entire microchip production until the 1960s, which later also enabled the success story of Silicon Valley.

And Germany must *thirdly* prevent the great dependence on important raw materials, which the country, unlike other industrial nations, has secured primarily through the cheapest possible purchases on the world market, but not through its own direct investments in the raw materials sector, by diversifying its own upstream and downstream value chains and connectivity. For all these challenges, not only a redefinition of Germany's role in the world is needed, but above all partners, in Europe and outside Europe.

Therefore, in the author's view, two principles must guide action: Firstly, for German security and economy, the European internal market is the lever to withstand the geo-economic power struggle between the US and China. Germany is an important trading partner for both superpowers. However, it can only throw its weight into the balance through Europe, as long as China, measured

1 Why this Book—Instead of a Foreword

by value creation, is similarly dependent on Europe as vice versa. Secondly, a continuation of the policy of equidistance towards the US and China, which has actually been pursued since the global financial crisis, but was then particularly intensified during the Trump years, is something Germany can afford as little as Europe can afford the temporary illusion of strategic autonomy. We must differentiate between the subsidy world champion from the East, who officially claims to adhere to international rules and the basic principles of international law, but constantly violates their spirit, on the one hand, and the hitherto most important ally on the other. There is, however, an imminent risk that the US under Trump will follow the path of autocrats and dictators such as Putin and Xi and Europe will be either forced to hedge economically and strategically between the great powers or truly become an independent global power on eye level with China and the US. And where rules are violated, their compliance should be demanded in the sense of reciprocity and equal treatment—this will be associated with higher short-term costs, but is not least in the interest of Europe's own credibility.

The book is intended and designed as a contribution to public debate in Germany. It is primarily aimed at the interested public and not at the professional world. While the topic of Ukraine has moved people in the country and has promoted a greater interest in foreign and security policy issues, global economic policy issues and debates are largely bypassed by most and are primarily led by economists and economic historians. Unlike during the Euro crisis, whose interrelationships rather overwhelmed society as a whole, the issues of supply chains, raw material security and technological change have now also reached the press and media, but for most the necessity of a paradigm shift associated with this in German foreign and foreign economic policy is still inadequately understood. This applies in particular to the increasing importance of using economic means to enforce (power) political interests—in other words, the new "geo-economics". The book aims to organize the scientific findings and debates circulating around this term and translate them into a language that "everyone understands". And it sees itself as a contribution of a political scientist with an economic background to debates primarily led by economists, recalling the (security) political element of global economic issues in the 21st century. In a world where both cannot be separated, this will hopefully lead to controversies over pointed theses and arguments.

References

Flach, Lisandra, J. Gröschl, M. Steininger, F. Teti und A. Baur: Internationale Wertschöpfungsketten – Reformbedarf und Möglichkeiten, Ifo-Studie für die Konrad-Adenauer-Stiftung e. V. 2021

Freedom House: Freedom in the World 2023. Marking 50 years in the Struggle for Democracy (March 2023)

McKinsey Global Institute: Global flows: The ties that bind in an interconnected world, Discussion Paper (November 15, 2022)

2

The Global Turning Point has Long Since Occurred

The world has radically changed in the last two decades, posing existential challenges to Germany and Europe. Since the global financial and economic crisis of 2008, the continent has been in a permanent state of crisis. Populism and nationalism, Brexit, and seemingly insurmountable differences on issues of migration, climate policy, and energy security, the reform of the Eurozone, and the improvement of European competitiveness in global markets threaten the cohesion of the Union from within. Not only since the Ukraine war, more and more people in the EU member states and in the US are feeling the negative effects of globalization or artificial intelligence through job losses, perceive democracy as fragile, and are worried about the future of health and pension systems due to demographic developments. Private and public debt is higher than ever. Rising interest rates to combat inflation carry more than ever the risk that shadow banks, so-called zombie companies, and state institutions go bankrupt.

At the same time, pressure from the outside is growing due to dictatorial Russia and a totalitarian China, wars in the Near and Middle East, and last but not least, the loss of trust in the transatlantic relationship after Trump's return to power.

With Russia's war of aggression against Ukraine, undoubtedly the greatest historical turning point in international relations since the fall of the Berlin Wall, this development reaches its sad climax. With it, Europe's foreign policy coordinate system, the institutional anchoring in the Western alliance under the protection of the US, has experienced a surprising revival under the Biden administration before it was shaken again under Trump. With all these developments and the additional threats emanating from cyber attacks, crisis prophets like the well-known economist Nouriel Roubini also see the Third World War already underway (Roubini 2022). This may sound overly gloomy, but it is certain that Putin's violation and Trump's ignorance of the basic principles and rules of international law challenge the liberal order in an unprecedented way. The invasion of Ukraine is primarily an attack on democracy and liberalism, which threatened to spill over from Ukraine to Russia and against which the regime in Moscow is resisting with all its might. Germany and Europe are thus not only threatened in terms of security policy, but also the foundations of their political order are at stake.

Europe's Late Awakening

Despite undeniable progress towards greater foreign and security policy sovereignty, the European Union has long underestimated the new geopolitical realities and settled in a world it believed everyone would follow on the path to a rule-based international order (Risse 2022). Integration, multilateralism, free trade, human rights, development, and peaceful cooperation were the cornerstones of a role concept understood as a "civil power," in which military power served as an *ultima ratio* at most and which both the European Union and Berlin elevated to the raison d'etre of foreign policy. Above all, the Federal Republic felt comfortable with this self-description, as it diverted attention from role concepts that located the country primarily as a self-serving export world champion and security policy free rider. At any rate, the normative idea of civilizing international relations through primarily non-military means seemed more attractive. And wasn't it more plausible from a German historical perspective?

After the peaceful collapse of the Soviet Union, Fukuyama's "end of history," the triumph of the West over Soviet ideology, described nothing other than the success story of the Federal Republic. Hadn't the US, especially Europe and Germany, become the norm for the rest of the world? Or, as Ivan Krastev put it so aptly in an interview about the Germans: "The German world was as the Germans saw themselves and others." A world on its way to what German intellectuals liked to call a post-imperial or post-heroic era. The number of democracies had increased worldwide, more and more countries were pushing into the EU and NATO. Russia and China were still far from being able to challenge the hegemony of the West militarily and economically. An unprecedented degree of global economic integration, increasing legalization and densification of international cooperation led the Federal Republic under all its chancellors since reunification to believe in the inevitability of the liberal order.

What was overlooked was that many of Europe's supposed integration advances had the opposite effect, that globalization brought economic efficiency gains but by no means the hoped-for political pacification of the world through increased interdependence, as Kant had promised in his treatise "Perpetual Peace." And that Europe can only become the global player it has been called for for years if it is itself crisis-proof and does not outsource security policy. Europe's, Germany's hubris consisted mainly in the last two decades in the assumption that its economic and political elites imagined the integration project as a linear process that did not know setbacks. And in the conviction that its citizens shared this narrative. This seemed to be the case as long as they felt the economic benefits of deeper integration primarily through the internal market project. The idea failed, however, the moment the added value of the political deepening of the integration project no longer opened up to Europe's citizens.

The End of German Illusions

The fact that Germany's ideal world could only thrive under the protective umbrella of the hegemonic power US was one of the unshakeable self-assurances that one believed one could afford despite all criticism of America. The idea that "security through renunciation of violence and 'critical dialogue' with dissenters" is fundamentally possible has been one of the axioms of German foreign policy since 1989. The absolute belief in these axioms was an expression of an identity that had been created after the Second World War and of which one was proud. This idea also became meaningful for European exceptionalism, and if it was mainly up to the Germans, it should also become meaningful for the rest of the world. Only in this way could one repeatedly deflect the accusation, already raised under the Clinton administration, of being a freerider who comfortably settled in this supposedly stable and peaceful

2 The Global Turning Point has Long Since Occurred

order and relied on Washington's security umbrella. And only in this way could one overlook the fact that most of the successor states of the Soviet Union returned to autocratic forms of rule after initial electoral successes of moderate forces and the Middle East sank back into chaos after the short-lived Arab Spring of 2011.

The second certainty, that "change through trade" is something like a natural law that all states in the world follow, also proved to be equally naive. Prosperity and a functioning market economy must be defended on contested global markets. The war in Ukraine also reveals a geoeconomic component. The response to Russia's aggression by China and India is not free from downright cynical reflexes, considering that Moscow's strategic calculus in the invasion was demonstrably based on the expected strategic and economic support of both. In this respect, China's strategic ambivalence in particular already represents a potential threat to Europe and Germany, which would have to respond with geoeconomic containment (sanctions) alongside the US in the event of a serious crisis. In the worst case, Beijing itself could seek to accelerate its decoupling from Western markets and the global financial system. Even if this is unlikely, one should not rely on Beijing not considering the associated burden on its own economy as an acceptable price for being able to pursue its own strategic interests more independently. Germany therefore also needs a foreign trade policy that begins with an abandonment of the "policy of appeasement" (Geinitz 2022) in dealing with China and ends with a more pragmatic resource and energy supply policy.

The war in Ukraine reveals the errors of a European energy policy oriented exclusively towards the cheapest possible supply and the principles of sustainability, which should have been disentangled from one-sided dependencies at the latest with the annexation of Crimea in 2014.

Energy security bottlenecks and resulting price increases will further exacerbate tensions between petro-states and consumer states (in Europe) that want to accelerate the transition to renewable energies, even without Russia's involvement. In the short term, the former will benefit from this development and fill their coffers with additional foreign exchange reserves, while in the medium term, the latter will likely gain the strategic upper hand by setting standards in technology, digitalization, component promotion, infrastructure, and equipment. The initial situation for consumer states is further exacerbated in the foreseeable future on the raw material front, where states like China own the most important rare earths and critical minerals and thus control the global supply chains (Hamilton 2023). For Europe, the value-added interdependencies with China in the fields of electrical engineering, textiles, and electrical equipment play an existential role.

The pressure in Europe, especially on Germany, to overcome its dependence on Russia and to set up the (European) energy mix as broadly and diversified as possible, increases immediately. This will not happen overnight, especially by concluding long-term cooperations and supply contracts with partner states from the Near and Middle East, the region of origin of fossil fuels,—in addition to the Gulf monarchies, especially Egypt, Algeria, and Azerbaijan (Engelkes and Schulz 2022); this also creates dependencies and is also associated with difficulties in terms of transport and infrastructure requirements. And as correct as it is to simultaneously push the transition towards solar and wind energy as well as green hydrogen, Germany must prepare for the fact that fossil dependencies will continue to exist during a transition phase that will last at least two more decades and therefore perhaps

2 The Global Turning Point has Long Since Occurred

even the unthinkable (temporary reactivation of nuclear energy and coal) must be considered.

The much greater challenge, however, is facing Europe, especially Berlin, with its dependence on China. The core element of China's policy of economic, technological, and infrastructural expansion is the targeted takeover of innovative technology companies and industries in medium-sized target countries like Germany. A decoupling will not be possible for an export nation like Germany. Even the majority of Americans shy away from such a move. Nevertheless, the mistakes made in dealing with Russia must not be repeated in the case of China—even if the dependencies are already much too large in certain areas. But at least two things should be considered in Berlin's future China policy: A strategic positioning in favor of the US is inevitable even under Trump, should there not be a reversal of the current course in Beijing or Trump indeed give up on Europe. And the previous practice of silently equating corporate and national interests is problematic when politics puts the security and independence of the country behind economic profit with the argument of not wanting to interfere in corporate decisions.

The Berlin turning point thus essentially takes place amidst an already apparent global turning point. It arrives, like so many other grandly announced foreign policy paradigm shifts of the country in the recent past, rather late and underlines the well-known reflexes of the self-centered, waiting, and only acting under pressure leading power in Europe. Like no other country, Germany has become accustomed to perpetual progress at the center of Europe since reunification and, as the largest economic beneficiary, has believed in the benefits of globalization. The primacy of the economy has always been the basis of the Federal Republic, and even in the 21st century, politicians and citizens of this country believed that its future lay in economic-ecological progress.

Hopes of the neighbors that the country would finally face the reality of a multipolar world and assume the leadership role assigned to it are based not least on the geographical proximity of the Ukraine war. In this context, the sociologist Andreas Reckwitz aptly spoke of the feeling of "political regression" and thus meant the regression to a political state long since repressed in German society—an offensive war in the middle of Europe, practically around the corner, threatening the European peace order. Suddenly it becomes clear that state action capability can still be a function of enforceable, often military power in the 21st century.

The current uncertainty and fear of the country is finally contributed to by the fact that this war makes the dependencies and prerequisites of our way of life so visible. The energy dependence on Russian raw materials, like the supply chain bottlenecks in connection with the Corona crisis, show how limited the decision-making options of politics and companies are in an open world economy and how quickly a reactive basic pattern has solidified in the political actions of governments. This fear is intensified by two further factors: on the one hand, the associated feeling of social decline extending into the middle class, where belief in the classic societal credo of further ascent through investment in education, work, and property ownership has long become fragile. On the other hand, the bitter realization that climate change and natural disasters are hardly manageable anymore. How we will live in the future, how we will move around, and what we will consume, according to climate researchers, will hardly have any impact on the magical 1.5 target for global warming, even with the greatest efforts in this country. Even with the greatest renunciation, they consider the number unattainable on a global scale. The same applies to the promises of alleged climate neutrality announced once again at last year's climate summit in Glasgow, the goal of not allowing more climate-damaging emissions by the middle of the century than can be removed from the atmosphere. Data already show that the target has become obsolete again after its announcement. So why give up cherished habits permanently? Why not follow those on the other side of the spectrum who unshakeably believe that the world will not perish even with warming above 1.5 degrees—even though the risks of severe climate damage increase with every decimal place. Taken together, these challenges are brewing into ever greater fears of loss in our societies, as we have probably not experienced since 1945. Peacekeeping in the 21st century therefore means more than just warding off military threats from revisionist autocracies from the outside. It means preventing and preempting global vulnerabilities for one's own economy that endanger the cohesion of societies, fuel populists, and distribute wealth gains even more unevenly. And it means building up industrial capacities in key technology areas and increasing resilience to global shocks such as the pandemic or global warming.

References

Engelkes, Simon, Ludwig Schulz: Raus aus Sibirien, rein in die Wüste. Nordafrika und der Nahe Osten als Bausteine in Europas Energie-Zeitenwende, KAS-Auslandsinformationen (Juni 2022). www.kas.de

Geinitz, Christian: Chinas Griff nach dem Westen. Wie sich Peking in unsere Wirtschaft einkauft, Beck 2022

Hamilton, Dan: Advancing Supply Chain Resilience and Competitiveness: Recommendation for US-EU action, Policy Brief, Washington 2022. https://transatlanticrelations.org

Risse, Thomas: Zeitenwende?, in: Internationale Politik (24.03.2022). https://internationalepolitik.de/de/zeitenwende-2

Roubini, Nouriel: Megathreats: The ten Trends that imperil our future, and how to survive them, Little Brown 2022

3

The Beginning of the Post-American Era

Europe, like Germany, stands at a turning point. It has been apparent since the global financial crisis of 2007/8 that strong international organizations and the few rules known to international law cannot contain geopolitical power claims, nationalisms, and revisionist thinking in terms of large spaces. Neither do the states that have benefited most from the opening of markets since 1989 (China in particular) accept the basic principles of the liberal order, nor are they really interested in its global spread (for example, through humanitarian interventions to enforce the same). Instead, they reduce the market under the primacy of politics to the greatest possible efficiency, assert their own order claims in their "spheres of influence", and at best develop a tactical-instrumental understanding of collective security systems like the United Nations. The pillars of the post-war international order, which initially also survived the caesura of the years 1989/90, are crumbling inexorably. Violent confrontations have now become the standard method for resolving interstate conflicts and within countries, while the multilateral security system slides into insignificance and the United Nations Security Council must helplessly watch as the principles and norms of international law are disregarded. At the same time, the gap between the global North and the global South is widening, with all the consequences of an ever-increasing debt burden, especially for the countries of the South, the exacerbation of the poverty problem, migration, and the associated strengthening of populism and authoritarianism.

The Return of Great Power Politics

The return of geopolitics, proclaimed by observers already during the Ukraine conflict in 2014 as a *first* global trend, describes a multifaceted phenomenon that cannot be reduced solely to the synonym for violent and ruthless power politics. American and British scientists originally understood geopolitics to be the analysis of political (and economic) phenomena that focus on geographical causal factors. And undoubtedly, the world is currently in the midst of a radical political system competition that is shaking all certainties for Germany. Russia and China are "leader states," as the long-time chairman of the Munich Security Conference, Wolfgang Ischinger, formulated, which have eliminated all counterforces in politics, society, and economy and, especially as nuclear powers, represent a geopolitical challenge for democracies. To become dependent on them increases the risk of strategic vulnerability. Therefore, their further rapprochement over war is the greatest geopolitical risk for the future from both a European and American perspective.

3 The Beginning of the Post-American Era

Putin's brutal war of aggression finally shows that systemic, geo-economic, and geopolitical challenges overlap and mutually reinforce each other today. With the invasion of Ukraine, the idea of pacifying the world through apparent system alignment and unlimited economic growth, from which everyone profited, recedes indefinitely into the background. Instead, national security, defense, and deterrence move to the center of political interest for all those states that have lined up behind the "Western alliance" in the UN Security Council.

It is astonishing how decisively those from politics, economy, and society in Germany, who until recently did not want to believe in the threat situation invoked by the Central and Eastern European neighbors for years, are now suddenly demanding a rethink. And yet, the turning point invoked by the Chancellor, as soon as it is proclaimed, already seems half-hearted again. Germany is struggling to find a stance on the new world situation. And it is especially struggling to find a new stance on Russia. Today it is clearer than ever: Germany's years of appeasement policy towards Moscow has made Russia stronger and Germany weaker.

Above all, representatives of the Social Democrats still see themselves in the tradition of the Ostpolitik as mediators and constructive partners rather than power politicians. The admission of the failure of the policy of "change through rapprochement" is visibly difficult. Until the end, they believed in the idea of societal and economic interweaving as a peace model. Putin's oft-quoted sentence about the collapse of the Soviet Union as the greatest geopolitical catastrophe of the 20th century fell early and revealed his imperial ambitions to restore a Russian empire. Behind this hesitation, there may always have been the fear of the "Russian bear" that one did not want to provoke. Even now, when Berlin has long been supporting Ukraine with military means, including the delivery of the long-tabooed battle tanks, it seems that it is afraid one could defeat Russia. In fact, former Chancellor Scholz prefered to say that the Ukraine must not lose.

But this attitude corresponded at least as much to the basic conviction that Moscow also believed in the formula of the indivisibility of European security, as long as the partnership provided one side with cheap energy imports and export surpluses and the other with technology and foreign exchange reserves. After all, the unrealistic view was that Russia also ultimately wanted the transformation to democracy and market economy as a prerequisite for stronger integration into existing European structures. Conversely, in Berlin, they were convinced that Moscow would therefore ultimately accept Germany's leading role in the eastward expansion of the EU and NATO—from which it is well known that it profited considerably economically and security-politically.

This view, as is now painfully apparent, was naive. It led to almost all governments and large parts of society persistently ignoring, since the collapse of the Soviet Union, the efforts that the West, led by the Federal Republic, repeatedly made to accommodate Russia's security interests and its "size and uniqueness" (Fritsch 2022). Whether it was the NATO-Russia Founding Act of 1997, Russia's admission to the G7 in 1998, or the Partnership and Cooperation Agreement with the EU in 1994, the "Strategy of the 'Four Spaces of Cooperation'" in 2005, and most recently the Modernization Partnership with the Union in 2010: all of them served the purpose of deepening the partnership with Russia and helping the country to diversify and future-proof its economic model, which was unilaterally focused on the export of fossil fuels. Equally ignored was what Berlin had refrained from doing since the 2000s, after initial enlargement euphoria in the 1990s, to support above all those countries that are now suffering most under the yoke of Russian aggression: It was Germany and France that denied Ukraine and Georgia not only NATO membership in 2008, but also at least compensatory support in building their own effective security and defense structures. Even the annexation of Crimea did not change the fact that Berlin still believed in a negotiated solution with Russia after the Minsk Agreement in 2015, when Moscow's intentions were already pointing in a different direction. In Berlin, violations of law by Moscow, such as the construction of the Crimean Bridge or the blockade of Ukrainian ships in the Sea of Azov in 2018, were met with appeasements regarding a tightening of the European sanctions sword against Moscow or stubborn adherence to Nord Stream 2. The governments under Schröder and Merkel had long since begun to put economic interests above all security concerns. In this way, they ultimately promoted a Russian policy that ostensibly aims at opening up spheres of influence, but is primarily directed against the political coordinate system of the West.

All of this was justified with traditional Russian encirclement fears, for which not only the greatest understanding was shown here, but to which the interests of the post-Soviet states were always subordinated after the big enlargement round in 2004. In all of Germany's political decisions regarding enlargement and Berlin's role as conflict manager, alleged Russian security concerns were the decisive independent variable in the past two decades and thus granted Moscow an implicit veto right with regard to the sovereignty of the accession aspirants. This is also why political representatives in Berlin found it difficult even at the beginning of the Russian invasion to acknowledge the high number of casualties in Ukraine and Belarus as a result of the German war of aggression during the Second

World War. Historical responsibility was always selectively focused primarily on Russia.

Only in this way can it be explained that since the beginning of this century, the geopolitical consequences of one's own actions could be ignored and it was accepted that Belarus joined the Russia-dominated Collective Security Treaty Organization with six former Soviet republics as early as 1992, or that Russian troops were stationed in the three European countries of Georgia, Ukraine, and Moldova over the years. Similarly it was ignored that all this happened against the will of the affected countries and, if one followed the Russian logic with regard to the eastward expansion, this policy was directed against the NATO border from the outset. And, last not least, that there was a persistent refusal to correct the central Russian narrative that there had been an agreement at the end of the Cold War not to expand the transatlantic alliance to the east.

It is true that the "Two Plus Four Treaty", contrary to all oral considerations that were made in this context during the negotiations on German unity in 1990, actually stipulated that German armed forces could indeed be stationed on the territory of the former GDR. But it is also true that there were no further agreements or prejudgments regarding a possible expansion of the NATO alliance to the east. They would have been null and void from the outset, given the fact that the negotiators of the Two Plus Four talks could never have anticipated the NATO alliance's decisions on enlargement—which are subject to the principle of unanimity in the NATO Council. Last but not least, those who repeatedly urged the alliance to show restraint towards Moscow must admit that neither NATO nor the EU followed any imperial logic in their enlargement, but that this was initiated by the affected countries themselves and therefore, for historical reasons, could never have been rejected by Berlin.

As correct as it was to try to include Russia in the European security order and international agreements, the signals from Moscow since 2007/8 were clear that Russia's willingness to integrate was always on Russia's terms. Putin was ultimately only interested in recognition as a major power on par with the West—a recognition that was explicitly denied to a weak EU in return. This was consistently overlooked, especially in Berlin and Paris. Thus, both the French vision of the liberal power EU as a strategically sovereign bulwark between China and a declining America, and the German idea of a cooperative, anti-imperial state system in Europe, in which Berlin and Moscow saw themselves in a kind of major power role for the stabilization of Eastern Central Europe have failed.

For Putin, from the beginning, it was about nothing other than the creation of a forward sphere of influence between Russia and the "old West". He never saw the country as a European eastern region, as many politicians did here, but as a large and independent geopolitical and strategic unit on a global level. Culturally, the country may still have been European, but politically it was "neither Asian nor Eurasian, but simply Russian", as Dimitri Trenin, one of Russia's leading foreign policy experts, has formulated.

Much suggests that even after Putin, the vision of at least partial restoration of the empire will continue. As in the past, when power changes raised hopes of rapprochement in the West, Russia is likely to find it difficult to break away from its autocratic and imperial traditions. At least this is more likely than a change of course towards democracy. This means that Ukraine, Georgia, and Moldova will continue to play a key role in Russia's strategic thinking. And it means that Russia will continue to keep an eye on the Baltic states, regardless of the three countries' membership in NATO. The decisive factor will be how much one can continue to rely primarily on American assistance. The states of Eastern Central Europe can feel reasonably safe, even if, according to Putin's imperial logic, NATO should also withdraw from Eastern Central Europe. However, if the the worst case scenario occurs and the US abandon Europe, those states would also have to fear for their security again and European states no alternative but to invest in a strong deterrent force.

For this reason, it is about nothing less than the geopolitical and geo-economic self-assertion of the continent—and thus the strengthening of its values in conjunction with the US. Germany plays a central role in this, not least because of its geographical central location—not as the "paymaster" of the EU, nor as a balancing power that conveniently mediates between the fronts on a global level and reaches compromises with France in Europe, or drives others before it (as in the euro crisis), but as a leading power that takes all member states with it. Europe's future depends crucially on Berlin providing the right answers to the dramatic structural changes and thus finally saying goodbye to fundamental premises of its foreign policy in the past. In the long term, it may be desirable that Russia's growing dependence on Chinese technology intensifies the isolation from the West and thus reduces the possibilities of influence on Russian society. However, peace and stability in Europe are likely to be possible for years not with, but only against Russia. The inevitable stronger re-focus on the integration of the willing-to-cooperate states of the eastern neighborhood, but also the Western Balkan states and the Black Sea riparian states, instead of the "Russia first" policy, is the best guarantee to overcome the centrifugal forces in European foreign and security policy between supporters of a NATO primacy on the one hand (Eastern Central Europeans) and "strategic autonomy" (France and Germany) on the other. And it is logical in terms of reducing Germany's overly one-sided economic dependencies compared to its European neighbors. Germany will have no choice but to strengthen the security and connectivity of its trade routes, especially in the extended Black Sea region towards Central Asia.

On the Future of Globalization

A *second* global trend and central component of this book is the simultaneous struggle of states to improve their national security also in matters of global supply chains, energy supply, critical raw materials, and foreign economic dependencies—a trend that already started with Brexit and Trump, continued under Biden's "buy American" policy and China's increased isolation policy, and reached its provisional climax with the Corona pandemic and Trump's return to power. Worldwide, protectionism and the use of economic instruments for power-political purposes are on the rise. Even in market economies, many are calling for an end to globalization, with serious consequences for economic efficiency and future price and inflation developments beyond the Ukraine war. States are reviewing their supply of food, medical products, energy, critical raw materials, and technology. Russia and India already restricted their grain exports before the Ukraine war, thereby exacerbating price volatility in agricultural products, Vietnam did the same with rice. At the same time, others (Egypt and Tunisia) began to fill the gap in the markets, thereby keeping their own economy afloat. Such developments increasingly compensate for the missing (power) means of multilateral institutions such as the UN, the IMF, or the WTO in dealing with global supply crises in the regions most affected.

With geo-economics, the use of economic instruments for (geo)political purposes, the end of globalization has not yet come, at most the process has slowed down. Nor does this mean that the economic doctrine that has been in place for decades, according to which overall economic gains from foreign trade can be achieved and everyone can be better off as long as profits are properly redistributed, is outdated. This is not changed by the restrictions that gains from foreign trade for large economies like the US are comparatively small and conversely potentially larger for smaller and poorer countries, and that there are always people who suffer losses in wealth due to foreign trade. From a macroeconomic perspective, protectionism always harms. The recent stagnation set in worldwide just as governments around the globe stopped their efforts to further liberalize world trade. The reintroduction of tariffs under the first Trump presidency has helped few Americans. Those who lost their jobs in the aluminum and steel industry due to the so-called China shock were primarily victims of the rigidities (lack of mobility, retraining and integration assistance) within the country that prevented the switch to other regions and sectors. In any trade war, however, short-term relief in one industry leads to likely job losses in other industries.

Two developments, however, are unmistakable regardless: On the one hand, the rich nations disproportionately benefited from the new technologies in the recent wave of globalization. These enabled internationally active companies to relocate their production, increase foreign direct investment, and exploit wage differences, often without having to disclose company-specific know-how.

As a result, according to the World Development Report, the largest companies in the global value chain contributed about 80% to world trade at the beginning of the 2020s. Trade disputes today are less and less about markets (Kappel 2022). The goal of the global champions is rather technological leadership in the sense of the ability to set global norms and standards in areas such as energy transfer, semiconductor technology, and operating software and to create dependencies. In this way, formerly isolated regions were also integrated into the world economy. Overall, however, production and consumption remained concentrated in just a few states. Among those who made the leap into the OECD circle were South Korea and Mexico, but also India and China, although the latter are still on the threshold. China in particular responded to this development with forced technology transfer in the context of joint ventures and thus also made the leap to a global economic power. This, however, simultaneously intensified the development towards mutual protectionism and de-globalization.

On the other hand, the trend towards the disentanglement of global economic and financial relations is obvious and is taking place primarily along the dividing lines between the political West and the authoritarian world. The above-mentioned strategic rivalry between the US and China is increasingly solidifying into a permanent global conflict constellation, which in the worst case can also result in a limited military confrontation between the two superpowers in the Pacific. At any rate, the geo-economic power struggle promotes a stronger concentration of international trade and harms cooperation.

According to WTO estimates, its members have introduced more than 1000 additional trade barriers in the last decade, including primarily tariff increases and import restrictions, thus significantly reducing global world trade.

Between the beginning of the pandemic and 2022 alone, the number of newly introduced protectionist measures increased by more than 30%, including not only tariffs, but much less transparent subsidies and export aids. While in the 1990s, goods exports grew on average more than twice as fast as GDP, export elasticity has been continuously declining since then, so that even before Corona and the war in Ukraine, global GDP for the first time since the 1980s exceeded global export growth. This means nothing other than that the degree of openness of the world economy is decreasing—by 15% alone since the financial crisis.

The consequences of these developments are particularly significant for export-oriented nations like Germany, but also for the trading power of the EU as a whole. They require an adjustment—not by decoupling from the Chinese market, as right-wing conservative forces in the US demand, but indeed in the sense of securing our own future against geopolitical risks. Europe and Germany will therefore also have to abandon the illusion that they can rely solely on alliances with like-minded states in the global competition between the two superpowers. Global markets remain vital for Germany and the EU and require strategic partnerships with those states that political scientist Parag Khanna locates in the so-called "Second World" (Khanna 2008). This consists of groups of states in Eastern Europe, Central Asia, Latin America, the Middle East, and East Asia, precisely those regions that have been central stages for the future shape of the world order since the upheavals of 1989/90. Here, it will be partly decided for the EU what the future balance of power between the three great empires of the 21st century, the United States, the European Union, and China, will look like. And certainly, this power struggle will not have a positive outcome for the Union if it, as in the past, adheres too one-sidedly to a norm-driven foreign trade policy, which recipient countries usually only follow to a limited extent.

The System Competition and the Change in the Global Balance of Power

This brings us to the *third* major structural change in international relations: the gradual end of a three-decade-long global order, also described as "Pax Americana" (Zakaria 2022). It is inextricably linked with the other two trends. The most visible sign of this is undoubtedly the economic rise of China, India, and other emerging countries, whose growth rates are significantly higher than those in the OECD area or the G7. If we take Gross Domestic Product in Purchasing Power Parities (GDP/PPP) as an indicator, then China, India, Japan, Germany, and the US continue to be among the leading nations. Nevertheless, the G7's share of global GDP has shrunk to less than 50% in just three decades. And while the EU, according to IMF projections, has prospects of keeping up economically and also increasing prosperity, its growth rates on average lag behind those of the US, China, and India (IMF 2022).

It is an irony of history that this development was the result of globalization, and that this in turn only worked because the US, as a hegemon interested in it, together with the Europeans, determined its rules and guaranteed its functioning. The economic historian Charles Kindleberger and the US sociologist Albert Hirschman coined the term "benevolent hegemon" for this connection of political and economic order as early as the 1970s, who, thanks to his military, political, and economic power, provides a liberal world economic order from which ideally everyone benefits. Following the logic of this theory, it was particularly worthwhile for smaller and weaker states to behave like free riders in such an order.

Signs of the erosion of Pax Americana are also the movements away from the "own" camp of strategic partners. The mere fact that the United Arab Emirates and Saudi Arabia, two countries that have been among Washington's most important strategic partners for years and depend on the American security umbrella in the region, refused to follow Washington in the vote on Putin's invasion in Ukraine in the UN Security Council during the Biden presidency, speaks volumes. The same applies to signals from Israel or India not wanting to break off political ties with Moscow. Turkey, which has increasingly become a central regional actor in recent years, has made it clear that its NATO membership does not prevent it from maintaining a special role in relation to Russia. This was already shown by the mutual recognition of the geo-strategic interests of both sides in Syria and Ankara's arms deals with Moscow in 2019. And this is becoming increasingly clear with regard to Turkey's current efforts to join the Shanghai Cooperation Organization (SCO). Ankara uses the new center of gravity in the Asian region both for stronger integration into China's Belt and Road Initiative and as leverage against the West.

No other country currently challenges the liberal order associated with America's long-standing hegemony as much as China does. The competition for global leadership has never been sharper, the stakes never higher. The goal of reversing the global pecking order and overtaking the US is the pivot of the radical change of course under the aegis of the most powerful Chinese state and party leader since the founding of the state by Mao Zedong. Domestically, it manifests itself in a return to Marxism-Leninism, long believed dead in Europe, and an unprecedented control regime that censors the internet and manipulates search engines, regulates internet companies, turns its own population into party informants through draconian laws and regulations, locks up and re-educates ideologically dissenting individuals (Uighurs), and swears society to its cause through the promise of "Common Prosperity" (Xi) by redistribution and curtailing the power of large internet corporations. Externally, the Chinese dystopia promises at best that the opening of the country will further increase the West's dependencies so that it simply cannot afford to decouple from China. Conversely, Beijing is increasingly disregarding the rules of the world trade system. Instead, the regime is trying to globally enforce its norms, which run diametrically opposed to Western values, by making these the standard for technical specifications for products and processes along the "New Silk Road" or by securing leadership positions in the International Organization for Standardization (ISO) and the International Telecommunication Union (ITU) of the United Nations. In this way, the hegemony of the US, which from Beijing's perspective is desperately resisting the inevitability of the Chinese succession, is to be broken.

As a result, the long-anticipated shift in geopolitical power relations led to a majority of states (141) speaking out against Putin's attack in the two votes on the resolutions on the Ukraine war. However, the relatively small number of countries (37) that abstained or at least refused to support the sanctions imposed by the West represents almost half of the world's population.

Russia will make every effort to use these power relations to its advantage and to further drive wedges into international cooperation. China and India will be the main targets of its efforts to counter the West's sanctions sword. In particular, the gas that Europe no longer buys is to flow to China in the future, and computer chips, cars, and machines that the West no longer supplies are to come from Beijing. The "foreign policy tandem," as Putin calls it, follows one main motive: The driving force for the strategic partnership from both perspectives is not mutual trade, but the common enemy in Washington and its attempts to create a unipolar world. To break Western hegemony, Russia therefore accepts the role of the junior partner, who has many nuclear weapons and can supply cheap gas, but is becoming increasingly economically dependent on Beijing due to sanctions and isolation by the West. Conversely, for China, Russia is a welcome disruptor that ties up the US outside its own sphere of influence in Europe (Ukraine) and the Near and Middle East (Syria, Libya).

All of this does not mean, conversely, that the emerging new global order must necessarily be a new bipolar one (US, Europe and their allies on the one hand, China and Russia on the other) or one directed against the US and Europe. There are too many undecided significant actors between the two blocs, whose positioning alternates. The idea of the liberal order is not at an end, but its achievements must be adapted to the new circumstances, both internally and externally (Neumann 2022). America remains the strongest power in the emerging new order for the foreseeable future, far ahead of the rest in almost all dimensions of power (military, economic, political, and cultural), with the exception of China (and parts of Europe), but no longer able to control world events as it did until the turn of the century. As the world's largest producer of hydrocarbons, however, the US benefits from rising energy prices, unlike its competitors such as China or the Federal Republic. Finally, Washington is likely to derive geopolitical benefit from China's delicate ambivalent stance on the war in Ukraine by forcing Europe to align more closely with the US and abandon its previous policy of equidistance between China and the US (Fröhlich 2021).

This is in Washington's enlightened self-interest, because the country today, more than in the times of the dream of a symbiotic American-Chinese relationship, relies on close partners. The global power struggle between the two superpowers is largely decided by the question of who forges the more reliable alliances. Therefore, it is correct that Europe, against the backdrop of the current global political change, contributes more to common security. However, this Europe is still vital for American security even if the current US president doesn't see it that way. Not because the US shares its own values and interests with no other world region as closely as with the old continent but rather because Trump, as his predecessors, claims to have the edge over China in the global power struggle.

The current power shifts in the global system do not necessarily mean that the future order will be a Pax Sinica. Geopolitically speaking, Beijing may indeed aspire to such an order with its claims to sovereignty over sea and land. With the world's largest navy, it is trying to push the US out of the Pacific, and with the Silk Road project, it aims to connect the opposing regions of Europe, the Middle East, and Central Asia across the vast landmass of Eurasia (connectivity strategy)—this large region now generates 70% of global GDP. On the other hand, the course change now sought by Beijing carries great risks for sustainable economic development. The pushback against the private sector, which now contributes three-fifths to the country's economic performance, coupled with an increase in state shares, does not bode well for the country's future. Therefore, it would be premature to write off the US again. They are still quite capable of a comprehensive containment policy. And the struggle of the great powers for urgently needed strategic partnerships or dependencies has not yet been decided in Beijing's favor.

Just as the Pax Americana once replaced the Pax Britannica, a power political restitution in the future will probably not occur due to globalization and worldwide economic interdependencies. The world is too complicated for that, the succession has become a simultaneous rivalry of states and no longer allows a new hegemonic order. The formation of the new order is not the result of the replacement of an old one, which is due to the weakness of the former hegemon. After two lost wars and a profound financial crisis, it is rather due to the US's desire for a break from world politics, even though history knows no breathing space. More than ever, the US also sees that survival in the future depends not only on world market shares, technological innovation, population size, and immaterial factors, but also on the ability to establish connections (connectivity) and forge alliances. Conversely, this means for countries like the Federal Republic, the end of the role of the free rider.

References

Fröhlich, Stefan: Comeback der Diplomatie, aber nicht der US-Dominanz, in: Politikum (Heft 2, 2021)

IMF (2022), World Economic Outlook 2022, Washington, D.C., Table A2–A4

Kappel, Robert: Die drohende Bifurkation der Weltordnung: der Abstieg des Westens geht weiter, Leipzig-Institut für Sozialwissenschaften (2022).

Khanna, Parag: Der Kampf um die Zweite Welt. Imperien und Einfluss in der neuen Weltordnung. Berlin Verlag, Berlin 2008

McKinsey Global Institute, Global flows: The ties that bind in an interconnected world, Discussion Paper (November 15, 2022)

Neumann, Peter: Die neue Weltunordnung. Wie sich der Westen selbst zerstört, Berlin 2022

von Fritsch, Rüdiger: Zeitenwende. Putins Krieg und die Folgen, Berlin 2022, S. 59

Zakaria, Fareed: Opinion: Putin's invasion of Ukraine marks the beginning of a post-American era, Washington Post, March 10 (2022)

4

The Geoeconomic Maps of the Future

The global geopolitical power struggle for spheres of influence is primarily conducted today through economic means. In the medium to long term, this development is likely as decisive for Europe and Germany as the question of their future defense capabilities. Especially for a country like Germany, which despite changing times will probably continue to struggle to assert its national interests by military means if necessary, the use of economic means becomes the most important instrument in the global power struggle. Even though the world is currently focused primarily on the war in Ukraine—military conflicts, despite all the conflictuality of the world and Putin's war inclination, are more the exception than the rule from the perspective of the West and its war-weary societies in the 21st century. However, the Russian invasion in February 2022 acted as a catalyst for the overlap of geopolitical and geoeconomic trends, especially in the area of energy and raw material security. The use of economic and financial instruments to expand one's power position in the global markets is certainly on the rise. This is particularly evident in the case of China. All of Beijing's "development initiatives" initiated in the last decade, from OBOR (2013) to the "Global Security Initiative" (2023) with the BRICS countries, primarily followed geopolitical and strategic motives. While the BRICS format initially served primarily developmental policy goals, it has now become a power instrument of China and Russia in international relations.

Governments worldwide resort to economic means to achieve their foreign policy and economic goals, but also to expand their spheres of influence. They thereby reinforce the trend towards nationalism, isolation, and increased readiness for conflict. The instruments used include not only the classic means of import tariffs or export barriers in trade policy, but also targeted sanctions in the areas of financial and monetary policy, energy and raw materials policy, and technology and investment policy (especially in the areas of synthetic biology, quantum physics, and AI). In all cases, these are protectionist measures that hinder the international exchange of goods, capital, people, or technology.

The Importance of Geoeconomics

The trend towards more protectionism, embargoes, and sanctions up to economic wars has always been a fundamental part of international relations. Only after the end of the Cold War did it enter the academic debate under the term "geoeconomics". At that time, the American military strategist Edward N. Luttwak (1990) described this turning point, which relativized the importance of interstate conflicts and the use of military means for exercising power in international relations in favor of the targeted use of economic instruments. In practice, however, the liberalization of financial and capital markets and the integration of emerging and developing countries into the global markets initially promised more growth and prosperity for all. For almost two decades, the world actually experienced consistently higher growth rates of world trade than of global economic output. This helped to lift a large part of humanity out of extreme poverty, but did not prevent the increase in inequality worldwide and the fact that globalization losers are left behind in all societies. Above all, the global financial crisis of 2008/2009 made it palpable in the West that networking also creates more dependencies and vulnerabilities that can be exploited to exert economic pressure.

Since then, the term, reinforced by the feeling that the world is simultaneously in a geopolitical power struggle for hegemony and system dominance, has taken on an increasingly negative connotation. Today, it no longer refers to the advantages of unrestricted trade and capital traffic. Rather, it refers to the political restriction that international trade is only good as long as it does not affect one's own security interests. After the terrorist attacks in 2001, the realization that internal and external security are prerequisites for freedom and state regulatory policy only gradually matured in Europe. In the US, however, foreign policy makers ignored questions of possible security policy consequences of open markets for far too long during the phase of excessive globalization. Only recently has the connection between external security and a functioning economic and social model dawned on both sides. The fundamental question today is: Can rivalry and economic integration coexist, and if so, what are the prerequisites for this?

The causes for the retreat of globalization are obvious. The main drivers are the uncertainties in societies since the financial crisis. From a European and German perspective, this was followed by the debt crisis, the trade war with Trump under his first presidency, and finally the supply chain problems exacerbated by the COVID-19 pandemic and the war in Ukraine, along with the tenfold increase in global transport costs that came with them. All these developments had a negative impact on trade, led to significant distortions in the financial and stock markets, increased the cost of imported products, and drastically reduced demand. The result: For most people, even in Western industrialized nations, the promise of globalization, the political pacification of the world through increased interdependence, has failed. Mutual dependencies in the form of trade and investment interconnections are no longer perceived as a stabilizing factor of the international system in the sense of a "win-win" situation between developing countries with lower price levels and producer countries with technical know-how. Instead, they increase the vulnerability and susceptibility to external economic pressure and promote a mercantilist zero-sum thinking. Even in the US, the driver of globalization for decades, free traders are now seen as an endangered species. It is plausible that this is easier with an export share of 10% of GDP (for Germany the share is 50%!) and given the size of their own domestic market with 50 states. Nevertheless, the protectionist sentiment in the country is worrying for two reasons: firstly, it overlooks the fact that cheap imports as part of sophisticated global supply chains give American households more financial leeway for other goods and services; the "Peterson Institute for International Economics" in Washington has recently calculated that the annual positive effect of trade amounts to almost 20,000 US$ for each US household. Secondly,

American protectionism inevitably rebounds on the world economy.

In addition, the power shifts in the global trade and financial system are accompanied by an increasing system conflict between the Western world and authoritarian regimes—a trend that is significantly promoted by different participation in digitization and technological progress on the global markets. Whoever controls the key technologies (AI, cloud computing, quantum internet, 5G) gains a security policy advantage. The same applies in the medium term in the energy sector for the power struggle between petrostates on the one hand and industrial states betting on renewable energies on the other. Russia's war in Ukraine shows how interdependence can be used as a weapon and forces entire societies to realign their supply chains overnight.

Worldwide, therefore, calls for boycotts against foreign countries are increasing and companies are beginning to consider shortening global supply chains ("near-shoring") and relocating production to trustworthy countries ("friend-shoring") or even bringing it "home" ("reshoring"). This development is reinforced by the dramatic influence of digitization on today's production processes and value chains; they are literally creatively destroyed and remeasured in the sense of Schumpeter's theory of economic development. Production becomes even less labor-intensive, with corresponding consequences for the labor market, regardless of demographic developments. Labor costs play an even smaller role in the choice of location. This will have effects on Western societies, insofar as mainly qualified and wealthy people will benefit—for decades there has been a decline in real incomes of employees without professional qualifications in the US. But it also has effects on the global markets: While digitization has so far been the driver of globalization and the interweaving of economies, the opposite development towards disentanglement and relocation now threatens, with dramatic consequences for those world regions that should actually benefit from worldwide division of labor and their demographic dividend. For them, this intensifies the feeling of a deeply unjust international order, which primarily protects the interests of the West, especially the US. Now they only benefit from the fact that China, Russia and the West are courting them more than ever before in history and are outbidding each other with "development policy" initiatives (Klingebiel 2022).

This has led to greater self-confidence and political emancipation in the affected countries, which allows them to play off external actors against each other due to a lack of political camp affiliation. At the same time, however, the new magic word in Beijing, Washington and Brussels is resilience. Resilience replaces efficiency, as enabled by global *just in time* production, and raises concerns in wide circles of the global South that all the well-meaning development policy projects will ultimately serve primarily the great powers' own interests. Even before the outbreak of the war in Ukraine, about 10% of German companies indicated in a survey that they intend to source more intermediate products and materials from their home country or the EU in the future, thus shortening their supply chains Flach et al. (2021). All this is happening at a time when the world economy is only growing moderately, inflation is rising and state debt is increasing, which further intensifies dependencies and vulnerabilities and increases the risk of conflicts up to military confrontations.

The American-Chinese Trade War

A debate has long been underway about who has primarily driven this trend. China sees the cause mainly in Trump's tariffs as a response to the trade deficit with China, which Beijing believes is primarily the consequence of chronic balance of payments deficits of the indebted US economy. It also points out that the volume of US direct investments in China accounts for just under 2% of the total volume of American foreign investments and that around 70% of American companies operating in China, according to surveys by the US Chamber of Commerce in Beijing in 2020, attested to an improvement in the implementation of intellectual property regulations by the Chinese leadership (Huang 2021). In the US, on the other hand, many blame China and its aggressive foreign economic policy. China, it is said across party lines in Congress, has benefited from the open markets of the West for decades, only to now shield its own markets from these in the transition to modernizing its economy through increased investments and a rise in domestic consumption. Thus, the total value of US goods trade with China in 2022 still stood at 690 billion US dollars, of which around 154 billion US dollars were exports and around 536 billion US dollars were imports. Therefore, at first glance, little has changed in the negative trade balance for the US despite tariff barriers since 2018, just as there can hardly be talk of a "decoupling".

The reasons for this are obvious. Both sides are aware of their mutual dependencies: Washington knows who primarily pays the US budget deficit and to whom American consumers owed low prices for end products and companies higher profit margins over the past decades. Beijing, on the other hand, needs the American sales market for its products and its export model like no other in the world. And both sides also know that an economic war, as the world is currently experiencing, costs jobs and prosperity (Siripurapu and Berman 2023). However, this does not seem to be an obstacle to both sides currently focusing primarily on confrontation and entering into a subsidy race that has serious implications for the global economy. America, China, and Europe are currently outbidding each other with billions in aid for the industries they consider to be future and security-relevant and which they see as endangered, knowing full well that subsidies create overcapacity, consolidate monopolies, drive up prices, and promote inequality. If such subsidies are also linked to export restrictions, production costs in their own country increase and export activity decreases. Nevertheless, all sides are currently either willing to pay the price for this or are convinced that they will emerge as winners from this trade war. This is the only way to explain how, since the global financial crisis in 2008, they have been able to launch approximately 18,000 subsidy programs for their industries in roughly equal parts, according to a study by the London Centre for Economic Policy Research.

The same argument can be made with regard to the discussion about the US trade deficits raised by Trump. Regardless of the question of whether trade balance deficits are bad per se and surpluses are good—this depends significantly on a number of factors and in the case of the US, the country has apparently been able to live well with it since the eighties, as most countries in the world still prefer to invest their currency reserves in the US, just as asset owners invest a large part of their money capital there. The deeper causes for the emerging trade war between Washington and Beijing lie in questions of security and systemic challenge, as we will see below. For these reasons, the complaint about unfair Chinese practices already under the Obama administration led to Washington regularly citing China before the WTO dispute settlement panel and imposing initial tariffs. The fear of losing one's own leadership role played a role in such accusations. Washington has since viewed China's economic and military modernization as a threat across party lines. The question of whether trade wars are winnable per se or reduce growth and prosperity for all parties involved is secondary. Economists have always debated this, with the majority opinion being that the latter is true and that trade wars basically only know losers.

Therefore, in the US, every protectionist outcry in the past was always followed by the realization that in the end trade restrictions were either not decided or were withdrawn after a short time. Tariffs, so the final credo went, might at best have a deterrent effect and the own income loss be small, but the risk of escalation is too great, especially in conflict with a system changer like China, as recent studies on the Sino-American trade dispute show (Evenett 2018). Afterwards, higher risk premiums, uncertainty and fears of the future in societies, which also affect investments in other, unaffected industries, ultimately lead to significant losses in GDP overall. According to calculations by some former chairmen of the Economic Council for the President, Trump's aluminum and steel tariffs against China and the European allies under his first presidency increased the profits and the number of jobs in the US steel industry, but at the same time they cost American taxpayers between 650,000 and 900,000 dollars per newly created job (Oermann and Wolff 2023).

Meanwhile, the feeling that has been latently noticeable since the global financial crisis has solidified in Western societies, that free trade not only creates winners all around, but significantly reduces the prosperity of certain industries and population groups, who therefore need protective tariffs. The flip side of the coin is job losses in the manufacturing industry, fear of selling off security-relevant technologies, and the loss of competitiveness of entire industries due to price-distorting currency manipulation on the Chinese side. In the US, therefore, a zero-sum thinking is increasingly spreading in political circles. Export controls, restrictions on direct investments, and counter-espionage are intended to stop China's ambitious technological goals. And of course, in Washington, there is a secret hope that the advantages of the greater demand power and elasticity of the US on the world markets compared to its trading partners will still be sufficient to come out ahead in the power struggle with China.

Even if this were the case, however, this development poses a great risk for the US economy and the world as a whole. In the 21st century, geo-economic interests cannot be enforced as easily for any economy in the world as they were during the Cold War with two closed political systems. The degree of technological and economic networking in the digital age does not allow this. Export controls and tariff restrictions worked in a world where technologies were based on manageable and controllable components. This is not the case for AI components and highly complex supply chains of today. The major tech companies that dominate the digital world not only have hardly manageable production sites, but also conduct their research outside the country.

In addition, the American and Chinese economies now have a similar order of magnitude, even though the American one is still significantly larger at given exchange rates of the currencies. This also creates dependencies for Washington on global supply chains and a network of companies and well-educated workers in the Chinese tech sector. Given more than three decades of sustained

4 The Geoeconomic Maps of the Future

growth rates of the Chinese economy, any extrapolation of economic development in China therefore appears threatening to Washington. The concern is less about the effectiveness of individual tariffs or other trade barriers. Nor is it about the extent to which their own industries can be kept alive, even though their problem is more structural, i.e., competitive in nature. The same applies, by the way, to the question of the use of other instruments such as sanctions, embargoes, boycotts, or development aid. The real concern for Washington, at least until Trump returned to power, was that Beijing would use its own retreat from the hegemonic role to shift the world away from a rule-based order towards a power-based order, together with Russia and other regional actors. Behind the American trade restrictions, therefore, were not only considerations as to the extent to which they can achieve economic goals or reduce their own costs. It was also about psychological, diplomatic, and security policy interests: To what extent can the behavior of the addressee be influenced in such a way that he will adhere to the rules of the international system, in this case the basic principles of the world trade order, in the future? Can own costs be necessary to underline the seriousness of the measures? Or is non-action the better option, even if it temporarily harms the sender more than the potential addressee, but in the medium term scores points with potential strategic partners due to greater reliability?

These are exactly the questions that have been raised since the competition between the two superpowers for the resources of the future and the future global supremacy escalated further with Trump's first presidency. Under Trump, the US for the first time equated economic security with national security, making it an integral part of American foreign policy. Like no other president before him, Trump has expanded US trade barriers against China and European trading partners—with massive impacts not only on the real production and welfare of the two great powers, but also on their trading partners. Laws such as the Foreign Investment Risk Review Modernization Act 2018 or the Holding Foreign Companies Accountable Act 2020 by the *Public Company Accounting Oversight Board* were intended to prevent takeovers of domestic companies or enable the exclusion of international companies from the stock exchange. In September and December 2020, the Department of Commerce restricted US sales to the Chinese semiconductor manufacturer SMIC on the grounds of a possible diversion for military end-use and placed the company on the Entity List, a list of companies and organizations that are considered a threat to the country's national security. At the same time, import tariffs on Chinese goods alone worth $550 billion were intended to correct America's balance of payments deficits. All these measures were justified by the fact that China's dumping prices were ruining its own steel and aluminum production and thus also threatening national security. In this way, Washington deliberately established a connection between trade and security policy, i.e., the economic and geopolitical interests of the US.

At the same time, the Trump administration undermined the principles of international trade and the role of the WTO. The target figures for bilateral trade agreed between the US and China in the Economic and Trade Agreement (2020) contradicted Article 1 of the GATT, which obliges WTO members to pursue a non-discriminatory trade policy. Finally, the US's policy of blocking the appointment of the appellate body of the WTO's dispute settlement body resulted in other member states being denied the opportunity to defend themselves against possible legal violations at the WTO level—a development that inflicted additional major damage on the already beleaguered WTO.

4 The Geoeconomic Maps of the Future

The biggest problem, however, was that Trump's ban also hit his own allies and since then the protectionist attitude towards them has not been off the table . The agreement reached with Brussels in 2021 to suspend steel and aluminium tariffs only briefly contributed to a temporary relaxation in transatlantic relations. Not only did Washington reserve the right to continue to impose a 25% tariff on German steel and aluminium exports to the US with the so-called "tariff rate quota" regime, should they exceed a certain threshold. Most recently, negotiations on ending steel tariffs failed miserably, bringing Europeans nothing more than a further extension of the suspension of protective tariffs until the beginning of 2024 and the bitter realization that the door to US subsidies for green technologies under the "Inflation Reduction Act" (IRA) remained closed to them.

Such an attitude also comes from a position of strength, which is not least due to the fact that the GDP of the US, unlike in the case of China or the EU, is only a quarter dependent on international trade, so the costs of an economic war for the country are considerably lower in relation to other countries. But it is above all an expression of the immense domestic political pressure that meanwhile any administration in Washington faces . Given the polarization of society and the radicalization of Republicans in Congress, Europe will also have to live with the uncertainty in the future that further concessions from the US may not be forthcoming, unless it positions itself more clearly than before in the Chinese-American power struggle and raises tariff walls against China in conjunction with Washington.

Nevertheless, America's pressure is associated with great political risks: Washington's isolationist policy towards China is advancing those in Beijing and also in Europe who, in turn, accuse the US of market manipulation through quantity rationing in the sense of "managed trade". The dilemma is that the willingness to use geo-economic instruments in trade, finance and technology policy makes it even more difficult to convince Europeans of the urgently needed stronger de-risking (notably not decoupling) and independence from Chinese markets. The goal of concluding a desperately needed free trade agreement with the EU, however it may be designed, is thus moving further away under Trump 2.0, even though an analysis by the US Chamber of Commerce already in 2021 concluded that US companies had missed valuable market access in both Europe and Asia due to the cancellations of TTIP and TPP. Washington is thus harming not only the urgently needed alliance in view of the geopolitical situation, but also its own economy.

At least the new economic policy doctrine formulated by security advisor Jake Sullivan under the Biden administration at the beginning of 2023 offered the chance for a transatlantic bridge in this dilemma situation. What is now known as the new "Washington Consensus" was nothing more than an attempt to adapt America's economic policy interests and dependencies to geopolitical realities. While the initial government statement in 2021 sounded as if it was necessary to confront the Chinese threat through isolation or disconnection, the new stance advocated risk minimization in economic relations with China—a formulation that has been adopted from Brussels and was supplemented by the concept of a broader "friendshoring" to include more countries than just the West. In this way, the European claim to keep global trade as open and rule-based as possible could best be reconciled with the need to set limits for China and reduce the risk of excessive economic dependence on the country. It is undisputed that the giant in the East has become the driving protectionist force in the competition for markets and global market shares.

No other country has used globalization as efficiently as China in the past two decades. Estimates suggest that the country's economic performance has increased by a factor of 30 since the opening of the world economy. An estimated 800 million people have escaped poverty, and China's accession to the WTO in 2001 brought about a rapid economic upswing. At the same time, Beijing has used globalization to extend its influence to every corner of the world. Geo-economic mega-projects such as the "New Silk Road" ("Belt and Road Initiative"—BRI) from 2013, Beijing's strategic investments in Africa and the establishment of the Asian Infrastructure Investment Bank (AIIB) founded in 2015 make China today the most important trading partner for more than 140 countries. With these initiatives, China is not only trying to drive the transformation of its own economy from an export-driven to an innovative and modern technology power by reducing industrial overcapacities in its own country and opening up foreign markets for Chinese goods. At the same time, the government in Beijing is striving for new rules in the international trading system to enforce its own interests. Europe, as the second pole of the BRI, as a buyer of Chinese products and location of highly developed industries, is a central geopolitical target in Beijing. Conversely, the Chinese market is the most important market and production location for many German companies.

The methods with which Beijing advances its projects have long since ceased to correspond to those of a controlled market economy, even though the leadership in Beijing asserts that it does not want to abolish globalization, but merely change it. For a long time, it seemed different, especially since the country appeared to be acting according to international rules on the surface. China's state capitalism did not operate with open protectionism in the form of tariffs or quotas, as is quite common in the West in otherwise free, privately organized markets. China's subtle state capitalism used other methods of financial subsidization and political support for its companies, largely hidden from the public eye, to compensate for their lack of efficiency. Internally, state-owned enterprises, private companies, and wealthy state funds worked efficiently together, unleashed entrepreneurial and innovative forces, and made the country not only the second-largest economy in the world after the US within just three decades, but also the largest creditor of the strategic rival with nearly 1000 trillion US$ through its export strategy and as the West's workbench, alongside Japan. Externally, Beijing primarily created economic dependencies with the Silk Road Initiative and politically instrumentalized these through loans, investments, bilateral raw material and trade agreements, and energy and infrastructure projects in Europe, Asia, Africa, and Latin America with a total volume of around 1.2–1.5 trillion dollars—an example followed especially by raw material exporters like Russia, who benefited from high world market prices, invested in strategically important industries and raw materials (especially oil and gas), and thus secured less private wealth than their own influence and accumulation of power.

Meanwhile, however, China under Xi Jinping has tightened its grip on the economy again, is pursuing an active industrial policy, and is increasingly isolating itself from the West (Geinitz 2022; Kroeber 2020). The goal is not to roll back, but to change globalization according to Chinese characteristics. However, this leads to the fact that foreign trade is gradually losing importance for China's economy. While it accounted for two-thirds in the immediate years after joining the WTO in 2001, it has now

4 The Geoeconomic Maps of the Future

fallen to around two-fifths and is thus significantly lower than in the US, for example.

China blames the West for this radical change of course, which in turn politicizes the economy and means "decoupling" when it talks about "de-risking". This may be partly true, but it does not change the fact that China itself is the originator of this development. For a long time, states and corporations that do not play by China's rules have felt the power of Beijing's leadership. National security and thus the preservation of its own power is the overriding goal of the Communist Party, with which deviators are pursued both domestically and abroad. And "de-risking" is essentially what the leadership in Beijing has been doing since it defended its positive trade balances against the outside world by all means. The result: Today, private entrepreneurship is only possible as long as companies adhere to the development plans and guidelines of the Communist Party, which the regime in Beijing has enshrined in its two long-term plans for the economic modernization of the country: the "Made in China 2025" initiative of 2015 and the "Silk Road" initiative. In both, the party leadership defines as its goal Chinese technological leadership by 2049 in 10 key industries, including robotics, information technology, transport, electromobility, renewable energies, and artificial intelligence (AI). In addition, China's president is striving for a civil-military fusion in order to better utilize synergies of "dual use" technologies such as AI and quantum computing for both military and economic goals.

The goals are to be achieved through self-development or autarky, isolation, and targeted company acquisitions abroad. Beijing wants to ensure that the country can serve ever larger parts of the global value chain and manufacture its own high technology in order to cushion sensitive sanctions that cut off its access to imports. Ready for this are about 2000 state-funded venture capital funds with a volume of up to two trillion US$. The list of American and European complaints is therefore getting longer and longer: While European companies are subject to state aid control both on the EU internal market and in third countries, Chinese companies are able to sell their products in Europe below market prices with the help of subsidies and advantageous credit granting. For years, Chinese company takeovers and investments in Europe have been following a strategic agenda, without the EU's regulatory framework offering sufficient intervention possibilities. Investors are particularly attracted by higher takeover premiums in critical infrastructure sectors such as energy or communication networks and in sensitive high technologies such as robotics or space travel. In the case of patents, Beijing severely restricts the rights of European companies to key technologies (such as 3G, 4G, and 5G) by having these used illegally or without appropriate compensation by Chinese mobile phone manufacturers. And when it comes to awarding public contracts, it is not uncommon for European companies to be not only disadvantaged, but even excluded from the Chinese procurement market through arbitrary regulations and approval reservations, while the previous practice in Europe grants Chinese providers free access. The sheer size of the Chinese market has made globally successful US companies like Google, Facebook, or Twitter accept considerable impositions and structural advantages of their Chinese competitors. In other words, China has been systematically violating the spirit and basic principles of the WTO for years: reciprocity and non-discrimination, especially most-favored-nation treatment.

Against this backdrop, it becomes clear that America's trade war with China gains its legitimacy and purpose less from protective or punitive tariffs aimed at improving its own macroeconomic position—economically, it has not unduly harmed China and has not benefited the US, especially since it has significantly burdened the alliance with partners and Washington's reputation. More crucial, and this also applies to Europe and Germany, as we will see in the next chapter, is that America's shift in trade policy is primarily rooted in China's aggressive trade, cyber, and technology policy, as well as its power claims, particularly in the Indo-Pacific. This is deliberately aimed at severing the connections between the technological superpowers and thus dividing the world into a Chinese and US-dominated tech sphere. The consequence would be two different types of technological standardization, separate supply chains, and the fragmentation of the internet. Google's Android operating system would no longer run on Chinese high-end products, and Europe and other world regions would have to choose one of the two sides or develop their own tech standards.

Such scenarios were hardly imaginable in the American tech industry until recently, given the fact that, for example, the entire Apple empire would not be conceivable without global division of labor with China and some other Asian countries playing a central role. However, the protection of one's own critical infrastructure, intellectual property, or technical know-how, especially in security-relevant sectors, the surveillance of other states or the export of corresponding technology to those with strategic dependencies, are today existential interests of every trading state. In this respect, it is also pointless to ask where, in individual cases, one can speak of fair or unfair practices. For the US, espionage in cyberspace is just as ubiquitous as the use of sanctions or control over the international financial system. The NSA manipulates and hacks hardware and software in the commercial sector and collects economic data. However, it has been justifying this so far by saying that it primarily serves the purpose of combating corruption and tracking illegal trade in dual-use goods. Or, that it wards off cyber attacks, as was first the case with Huawei in 2007, when Washington preemptively manipulated its hardware and software to decrypt security threats emanating from it.

China's ambitions, on the other hand, go further. It is deliberately waging a trade war in the sense of targeted unfair laws and administrative practices, sponsored or launched by the state, which are directed against Western companies. And just as undisputed is the political intention associated with such measures to weaken the West or replace the international order shaped by Washington. In this respect, the threat lies in the merging of previously separate areas such as security, economy, and order. And in this respect, China must be seen as a revisionist power, which is simply not interested in the principle of peaceful coexistence still unabashedly propagated by the leadership, but wants to replace the existing global order with one that corresponds to its own ideas. As early as 2013, the Communist Party of China identified the danger of Western ideas and concepts as being directed against its own country, which should be combated through targeted intimidation of foreign governments and companies—through forced diplomacy, trade and investment sanctions, boycotts or arbitrary arrests, up to state threats in case of undesirable behavior or to enforce territorial claims, as they are primarily registered in the Indo-Pacific (Rudd 2022). China's geostrategic map today not only includes the areas of Arunachal Pradesh and Aksai Chin traditionally claimed by India, but also Taiwan and almost the entire South China Sea; Malaysia, the Philippines, Indonesia, Brunei, and Vietnam are equally affected by Beijing's arbitrarily drawn "nine-dash line," with which China marks its claims in the maritime area.

4 The Geoeconomic Maps of the Future

For Washington, it is primarily about its own technological leadership and security, and about the impending geostrategic loss of power in the affected regions. Since AI, deep learning using artificial neural networks, and cyber technology (information warfare) are used today not only in the military sector but primarily originate from the commercial sector, thus representing dual-use goods, there is a close connection between globalization and national as well as international security. And where Chinese tech companies demonstrably support Beijing's military modernization with their software, investment and export controls towards Chinese companies with connections to military and surveillance technology are as necessary from Washington's perspective as the "Chips and Science Act of 2022", with which the Biden administration planned the development and production of American semiconductors and computer chips. Such a policy of "de-risking" does not mean decoupling from China—nor does it mean containing Beijing. Both would only harm their own economy, just as Beijing is currently harming itself most with its isolation plans and the choking off of private investments. Rather, the US strategy aims to present the country as a better alternative, and as a still open market also for Chinese products. The US pursued such a strategy also in the 20th century to successfully fend off system competitors. During the Great Depression, it was far from certain that the US economy would overshadow the fascist regimes in Europe, and Washington also experienced periods of weakness and doubts about the principle of open markets during the Cold War (Posen 2023). In the end, however, the US always prevailed by sticking to the principle of competition. For this reason, the EU should not immediately escalate US measures such as the "Inflation Reduction Act" of August 2022 into a new trade war with Europe, but rather set the course for closer cooperation with the US with its own "Chips Act" within the framework of the "EU-US Trade and Technology Council". Nor should Europe immediately rebuke Trump's proposed "Faior and Reciprocal Tariff Plan", signalling that Washington is willing to destroy the global trading system. Rather Europeans should at least signal their willingness to discuss purchases of LNG and defense kit, provided that the US does not completely abandon Europe as is now threatening in the case of Ukraine.

The Shift of World Trade Towards the Global South

The American-Chinese trade war has massive effects on the world economy and global trade. The world we live in is no longer one where the primary goal of all economic activity is the most efficient production processes at the most cost-effective global locations. The rule-based world trade system WTO as a motor and control instrument of global trade is in ruins and is unlikely to recover quickly. It was based on agreements by largely liberal democratic states of the West, which believed in the market economic principles of private entrepreneurship and the price mechanism—principles that China, as the biggest system challenger but a member of the WTO, does not share, and that now are very likely to be given up by the US administration as well.

It was therefore only a matter of time before the order that had grown over decades and the international organizations that have supported it since 1945 would reach their limits, especially since the West also contributed to this. One can imagine how the regular withholding of important medicines in Africa with Western references to WTO regulations on patent protection in the so-called

4 The Geoeconomic Maps of the Future

Global South is received. And the fact that America and Europe still protect their agricultural markets, even though the WTO rules expressly allow preferential agreements deviating from the "principle of reciprocity" with third countries, is as much a disgrace as the fact that the WTO has not been able to dismantle the hierarchies within the member states to this day due to Western resistance. After all, the US has been blocking the dispute settlement mechanism since 2017, ensuring that the only functioning mechanism in favor of countries of the Global South can no longer be used.

The consequences of these developments are devastating, as they also impact other international organizations. The return of great power politics is now also paralyzing the United Nations, whose loss of significance has become increasingly apparent over the past decade. Since the Syrian war, Moscow and Beijing have blocked several UN resolutions against the Assad regime and used the withdrawal of war-weary America from the Middle East to increase their influence in the region. The UN Security Council has been completely blocked at least since Putin's intervention in Crimea. With the open neo-imperial policy of Russia and China, international law is left by the wayside and the Security Council has become the stage for an anti-Western sentiment of the Global South, mainly led by Moscow. This trend has visibly intensified as a result of the terrorist attack by Hamas on Israel. Within a short time, Israel's retaliatory reaction led to a reversal of the victim-perpetrator role, with Israel being declared by most emerging and developing countries as a neo-colonial outpost of the US or the West. Last not least, the US under Trump has shown its contempt for the organization's lack of efficiency.

To the extent that the UN or WTO have lost their role as pillars of the liberal international order, all participants are resorting to alternative formats and further eroding multilateralism. While the West dreamed of global "alliances of democracies" under Biden to maintain a value-based and international law-based security architecture, emerging countries seek their salvation in the BRICS format dominated by China and Russia, hoping for a "fairer order" promised by Beijing and Moscow. In the case of the WTO, the balance of power weighs differently. Faced with the difficulties of asserting its interests in the World Trade Organization, the West is resorting to bilateral and plurilateral free trade agreements or inter-regional agreements, which are often perceived in the Global South as a "second-best solution" because the agenda continues to be primarily determined by the major economic powers US and Europe. This is also why it is the emerging countries that still predominantly adhere to the WTO (Plagemann and Maihack 2023).

The fragmentation of the global order is further intensified by the above-mentioned increasingly clear emergence of three separate regional markets in the course of the power struggle between the US and China: one centered around the US in the Americas; an Asia-Pacific market dominated by China; and finally a European one, provided the weight of the EU-27 as a whole is taken as a benchmark—with all its influence towards the eastern part of Eurasia.

This trend undoubtedly strengthens China above all. The reason for this is simple: Asia is definitely the region with the best growth prospects in the coming years. 9 of the 10 largest ports through which world trade runs are located on the continent. And most of the hubs for Asian trade are in China. Trade of the countries of the Asian Association APAC now accounts for a third of global GDP, with a rising trend. In other words, whether in India, Indonesia, or Vietnam, growing middle classes in these countries are buying goods produced on the

4 The Geoeconomic Maps of the Future

continent, with online trade likely to become the biggest growth engine in the region. Thus, these countries are following China's pattern—moving away from an export-oriented growth model towards consumption.

The emergence of separate regional markets is overlaid or supplemented by the struggle of the three major economic blocs for the favor of the undecided states of the Global South and on the periphery of their respective spheres of influence in Central Asia and Africa, in the Middle East and partly in Latin America. The fact that these states are no longer merely pawns of the great powers, but on the contrary determine or drive up the prices for strategic partnerships, is also part of the new geopolitical realities. This development is particularly painful for the West. What is perceived as a loss of influence in these countries is seen there as a gain in political, economic, and cultural autonomy. Especially in the area of the global economy, the balance of power has continuously shifted at the expense of the West over the last decade. India has now become the largest consumer market and the fastest-growing economy, China the most important trading partner for the majority of states worldwide. South-South trade is thus more extensive today than North-South trade, which in turn leads to the countries of the Global South trading more with each other than with the industrialized countries of the West and that trade with developing and emerging countries is at least as important for the West as North-North trade among themselves (Mold 2023). As a result of these developments, Chinese state-owned companies are now majority owners of European ports, Asian countries are the largest buyers of oil and gas from the Gulf states, and Indian entrepreneurs are hard to imagine without in British industry. The majority of Brazil's agricultural exports go to China and not to the West, and Putin has become Beijing's largest supplier of oil and gas. Even the traditionally mainly Europe-dominated African market has now become a coveted target for Indian, Chinese, and Turkish companies, because there they do not share the obsession with the Chinese debt trap as long as infrastructure projects achieve faster and more concrete results than Western alliances, whose normative requirements continue to be perceived as political patronage.

Neither economically nor politically is this power struggle lost for the West. However, it should not be conducted with the claim to absoluteness, as has been superficially done in the past—even though good trade relations were maintained with those very countries, such as Brazil, India or South Africa, which were still referred to as value partners when they had already become increasingly autocratic. This was not well received in many parts of the Global South. The West is feeling the consequences today in its efforts to forge a global defensive alliance against Putin's war in Ukraine. The accusation of double standards, hypocrisy, and lecturing rings out loudly: one invokes international law and norms when it suits, but conveniently overlooks one's own rule violations when one's own interests are affected. The criticism culminates in the narrative cultivated by Moscow and Beijing that the rule-based order is nothing more than an increasingly ineffective instrument for enforcing Western hegemony (Kleine-Brockhoff 2023).

One should not follow this narrative, but one should admit that the interpretations of a missionary liberalism of the past three decades have failed - and are at least one reason for the rise of *Trumpism* in the US. This applies to both the offensive American variant, according to which Washington wanted to carry democracy out into the world in a Wilsonian manner, and to the European interpretation, according to which the world would follow the

4 The Geoeconomic Maps of the Future

example of the European unification process in the spirit of Jefferson. This does not mean that one should not continue to insist on the principles of the liberal order and defend them against autocracies. But it does mean, above all, to scale back one's own claims towards an expansive universalism and to recognize the increased importance of the countries of the Global South outside their own regions and to understand their efforts for pragmatic balancing of interests. Example India: There, they share the American concern about the growing Chinese influence in the Indo-Pacific and a too strong rapprochement between Beijing and Moscow in the course of the war in Ukraine, but at the same time India is an active member of the BRICS. The relationship between Russia and China is not without tension, as their competition for supremacy in Central Asia shows. Instead of betting that the countries of the Global South will form a united front against Russia and China or even carry sanctions against them, one should remember that most of them are indeed supporters of multilateralism and the basic principles of the UN. This does not exclude that they pursue their own strategic interests vis-à-vis the superpowers, play them off against each other and want to profit from their offers. Others—especially oil-producing oligopolies—create dependencies or fall into the sphere of influence of a superpower due to their weakness. A third group of states forms coalitions with emerging empires (like China) and thus challenges the traditional superpowers (US) for their leadership role. They all have in common that they, like China and Russia, already see themselves in a multipolar order in which they force the major powers into a geostrategic competition for the favor of future alliances—with quite different foreign policy means: while the US relies on coalitions, financial support and security partnerships, Europe offers development aid and approximation to the internal market against corresponding reforms. China, on the other hand, lures with loans and infrastructure projects.

What is happening at the meta-level is already a reality at the micro-level. Companies worldwide are now adjusting to a changed, fragmented world in which more flexible bi- or plurilateral arrangements dominate and in which geopolitical conflicts increasingly determine corporate decisions. What we are experiencing is the devolution of the global economic system in a way that globally operating companies have not known before. According to a survey for the "Harvard Business Review", the authors conclude that the vast majority of American CEOs see their companies entangled in political and social issues today, that they must play a more active role in shaping labor law, environmental or intellectual property rights issues, and that they perceive the boundaries between civilian and military activities in the areas of critical infrastructure, communication services, energy security as increasingly opaque (Charan and McGrath 2023).

In the Shadow of the Superpowers—Europe's Dilemmas

How can Europe position itself in this power struggle? What role can it play to defuse this power struggle? Only recently has Europe been trying to counter China's isolationist policy and expansion of its geo-economic sphere of influence, well aware that it can strengthen its own ability to act, but a European IT world largely independent of China and the US is unrealistic in the short to medium term. Europe has watched China's rise to technological power for far too long, while at the same time making itself dependent. The dependency is now turning into an almost fearful defensive posture, instead of playing its own trump cards or perhaps even learning from China. If one had looked more closely, one would not have missed that China has been promoting its electric car industry, among other things, for a decade and a half, taking advantage of its own, less fragmented domestic market compared to Europe. Europe's attentism has thus practically invited Beijing to create critical overcapacities first in solar and wind energy and now also in the field of electric cars, which can certainly cause problems for the country. China could today produce about twice as many electric cars as are sold in the country, which further increases the pressure on the European sales market. The reduction of such overcapacities also became a decisive driver of the Silk Road Initiative.

Meanwhile, the Commission, under its President von der Leyen, has become the driving force to stand up to China, the US, and other emerging countries. Brussels has learned from Trump, COVID, and the Ukraine war and is not only stepping up rhetorically. After all, there is now something like an overall strategy of the EU to protect its own competitive position on the global markets. With the EU's "Investment Screening" regulation (2020), it is now also possible for Germany, after amending its foreign trade regulation, to control and, if necessary, prohibit company takeovers from third countries. With the "International Procurement Instrument", the EU Commission has for the first time proposed a legal framework for access to the EU procurement market, which also serves as a bargaining chip for negotiations with countries to open their markets. The same intention is pursued by a legislative proposal by the Commission to combat competition-distorting state subsidies in the future. Finally, the EU supports the G7 initiative "Build Back Better World" (B3W) from June 2021, which aims to stimulate private investment in infrastructure projects in developing countries, to counter China's Silk Road initiative.

The transition from an economically driven to a more foreign policy and geopolitically motivated foreign economic policy is more difficult for the EU than for the US for several reasons, where even under Biden there was no intention to move away from the geo-economic containment of China: *Firstly,* as a region that is more dependent on international trade than any other worldwide and therefore insists on adherence to the principles of openness, the EU cannot afford to decouple from the global sales markets. Just under 16% of global exports currently go to the EU27, followed by China and the US with just over 10% each. And also in terms of imports of goods and services, the Union is again just ahead of the US and China worldwide with around 13% (EU Statista 2022).

Secondly, while China policy in the US is one of the few uncontroversial fields in Congress, the Union, not least because of tough coordination processes and differences among the member states, repeatedly reaches its limits regarding a uniform China policy. This is due not least to different dependencies of the member states on China. France, Italy, and Spain export just half of the German volume of goods and services to China. The revenues of German large companies in China amount to 6% of German GDP, twice as much as the six strongest economies after Germany generate together. It is logical that people in Berlin think differently about "de-risking" or even "decoupling" than elsewhere in the EU.

Thirdly, not all member states in the EU share the majority skepticism among Republicans and Democrats in Washington regarding China's threats to annex Taiwan along with the globally most important semiconductor producer TSMC. There is no talk yet in Europe of a turning point regarding a boycott of Chinese key industries in the technological and software sector, as Washington is pushing for. The recent sanctions, with which Washington has imposed export controls for the delivery of microchips and highly specialized machine tools for chip production and also prohibited Americans and green card holders from participating in the development and production of microchips, could hit the Chinese economy hard, as they are not only directed against individual companies like Huawei, but against an entire industry including artificial intelligence. For the first time, not only commercial but also military interests are affected by the sanctions. And thus, under Biden, the American challenge even went beyond the measures of his predecessor Trump. People in Brussels may be that far, but elsewhere, especially in Germany, they still find it difficult to see China as a security threat.

Fourthly, Europe also has more to lose than the US with a "de-risking" strategy. Chinese companies are by far the largest suppliers of goods to European consumers compared to the US, accounting for almost 20% of all imports into the EU in the first half of 2023 alone. The dependence on the production of lithium-ion batteries, which is so important for the European energy transition, is even 80%. The dependence on investments is somewhat less critical, but considerable: Since 2010, China has consistently bought into European infrastructure, whether in ports (in at least 10 countries), power grids (especially in Portugal, Italy, and Greece), or underwater telecommunications cables ("peace cable" from Pakistan to France). Even though the investment volume has decreased in the last three years due to the restructuring of the Chinese economy towards the self-development of top technologies, it remained at a high level of around 25 billion annually between 2020 and 2022.

Fifthly, the EU's ability to win over European companies for its initiative is limited. After all, it is up to the latter to implement the plans in the end. This will likely require not only political persuasion, but above all appropriate financial incentives or public investment programs. Few EU states have the necessary fiscal leeway for this. Conversely, the threat of subsidy withdrawal or even sanctions in the event of overly careless business dealings with China by certain European companies does not seem to be the solution, as this could not only weaken the European economy as a whole, but also encourage companies to relocate from Europe—not to mention that such a policy would have to be implemented by the member states, which in turn would lead to distortions between the economies.

Sixthly, the creation of European instead of global supply chains is unrealistic in the short term. US companies control the technology for building advanced semiconductors, giving them a significant strategic advantage in relocating necessary supply chains to the US. Europe is miles away from this and thus remains dependent on the US in this technology sector. This is also why Brussels' efforts towards "de-risking" or greater independence from critical technologies are not very promising in this area. The same applies to other critical goods outside the semiconductor industry: Especially in the case of raw materials and critical minerals, the situation in the chemical and electrical industries, but also in mechanical engineering, will even worsen for the EU if it does not free itself from unilateral dependencies and quickly looks for alternative sources and technologies and uses its own niche capabilities as a lever. This is also why the Commission, not least in response to supply shortages, especially of medicines during the pandemic, identified critical dependencies for Europe for a total of 137 products in six economic sectors in 2021 and subjected them to a stress test (including raw materials, batteries, pharmaceutical ingredients, hydrogen, semiconductors and cloud technology) and called on member states to develop proposals for activating European supply chains (European Commission 2021).

The result was sobering. The Union is dependent on imports for between 75 and 100% of most metals. Of the 30 raw materials that the EU classifies as "critical", 19 are mainly supplied from China alone. These include magnesium, where China almost has a monopoly (93%), rare earths (98%) and bismuth (93%). These raw materials are essential for the digital and green transformation planned by the Commission (Flach and Teti 2021). While many of the critical raw materials have long gone into electronics and semiconductors, batteries and green technology are now being added. In addition, the urgently needed high-performance chips in the semiconductor sector require more and more elements from the periodic table, as long as societies are not in an efficient recycling economy. By 2030, the EU estimates, the demand for cobalt alone will be five times as high as it is now. Over the same time horizon, the EU-wide demand for nickel for the production of lithium-ion batteries needed for e-mobility is expected to increase eightfold. If the Commission's plan to meet this demand in part by having the EU produce 10% of the annual demand itself and refine 50% of the resulting critical raw materials were to be implemented by then, one can vividly imagine the Europe-wide outcry from climate activists in view of the environmentally damaging consequences of their extraction.

Does this mean continue as before and trust that China will continue to supply in view of its own dependencies and vulnerabilities? No—all this should not prevent Europe from making the course change announced by Brussels, especially towards China (Johnson 2023). As the last point shows, the risk of political blackmail is far too great. In Beijing, efforts will continue to be made to boost domestic consumption and reduce the country's export dependency. The aforementioned concept of "dual circulation" is intended to set the future direction for China's economy and make the Middle Kingdom less dependent on trade with the US. And, if necessary, also from Europe. Whether the desired vertical integration of the economy is successful is another matter. It is also not to be ruled out that the bottlenecks resulting from this in the aforementioned key industries will negatively affect growth potential (Garcia-Herrero 2022). At the moment, the radical shift towards more domestic consumption and less investment in infrastructure, as well as the pandemic, are having a negative trend impact on the economy. Given the gigantic debt of local governments, collapsing corporations and shadow banks, and high savings rates, growth rates of 4% instead of 7-8% for the economy are now considered realistic.

However, it is certain that the highly uncertain development in China will hit Europe's economy. The fact that it has not yet explicitly become the target of Chinese countermeasures is due to Beijing's calculation of wanting to drive a wedge between the transatlantic partners once again. Like Washington, at least until recently, Beijing understands that the struggle in the world markets can only be won by forging strategic partnerships; they decide who will ultimately have the upper hand in the battle of the superpowers. For this reason, the EU must reduce its

4 The Geoeconomic Maps of the Future

dependencies and support its own industry more strongly. This is now the majority view among societies in the member states, including Germany. If action is not taken now, Europe risks being left behind or marginalized in this zero-sum game between the economic superpowers US and China. And it would always be strategically sensible to reduce these dependencies at a time when China still needs Western markets and technology unchanged. Only in this way can Europe's geoeconomic potential be used as a political lever.

It is clear that the partnership with the US plays a central role in this. Even now, Beijing's Silk Road initiative can only be countered in the transatlantic alliance (Pisani-Ferry 2021). Beijing's world's largest foreign exchange reserves, which are still largely invested in American government bonds, can only be matched financially with a joint effort. At the moment, both Washington and Brussels are mainly relying on the insight of the recipient countries of the mega-project that the promised welfare gains for all will likely come at a high price in the end. China's investment policy is tied to political conditions that create dangerous dependencies. Contracts are usually opaque, grant only repayable loans, and often explicitly exclude debt restructuring. After ten years, there are increasing defaults amounting to almost 80 billion dollars, which Chinese credit institutions have to write off or renegotiate. In more and more cases, it becomes clear that recipient countries cannot pay the market interest rates demanded by Beijing. In addition, many infrastructure projects are neither economically sensible nor sustainable, as Chinese development banks are obliged to acquire projects at any cost under pressure from the political leadership in Beijing.

From the "Brussels Effect" to "de-risking"

In principle, the dependency, as in the case of Germany (see following chapter), is portrayed all too much as one-sided. In fact, when it comes to value-added import and export shares in trade, China is still somewhat more dependent on the EU than the EU is on China. Regardless of this, just 2% of the total value added in EU end consumption comes from China, and on the EU export side, 2% (for Germany 2.7%, mainly in the areas of chemistry, electrical industry, mechanical engineering, and metal products) of the total EU value added goes into Chinese end consumption, as a study by the German Economic Institute recently calculated (Matthes 2022). Almost 75% of all German industrial goods, where dependencies exist, however, come from EU member states.

With the internal market and its nearly 500 million consumers, the EU does indeed have an economic lever that it can also use as a powerful tool of foreign policy, without giving up the principles of openness and sustainability. As the still most important trading partner for many countries (most important export market for the US, India, South Africa or Russia and second most important for China and Brazil) and the world's largest development aid provider (more than half of all money for global development aid) with a GDP per capita three times as high as China, it can exert considerable influence on the setting of international norms and standards for goods and services.

This so-called "Brussels Effect" (Bradford 2020) means that the EU can extraterritorialize its own regulations and norms and thus expand its sphere of influence. This can be observed particularly in the case of the General Data Protection Regulation (2016), which forces all cloud service providers to implement the high EU standards for the protection of personal data in accordance with Art. 28 of the GDPR. The tech giants from the US, Japan or South Korea voluntarily align with these standards in return for access to the EU internal market, in order to avoid the otherwise higher adaptation costs caused by linguistic, cultural and legal differences between the individual EU countries. Google makes its billions in profits mainly in Europe (market share 90%), Facebook has more daily users in Europe (almost 280 million) than in the US. Meta and Apple, as the largest providers of cloud computing services, generate 22% and 24% of their revenues in Europe (for both, after the US, the most important market). And other large tech companies also list Europe as their most important foreign market in their annual reports. For all of them, the European internal market, with an import share of 30% of all global services, is simply too significant for them to afford to ignore its legal regulations. Unlike in the goods market, service providers cannot easily compensate for the loss of sales markets on other markets. Technology companies that threaten to leave the market or not introduce new services in Europe usually back down relatively quickly.

Europe's regulatory power in the digital sector is also evident in the EU Cybersecurity Act (2019), which for the first time creates a uniform framework for the certification of information and telecommunications products and services, and in the Artificial Intelligence Act (2021), which adopted the world's first legal framework for this key technology. Finally, the EU sets global standards with its chemical regulation, in climate policy, where the planned CO_2 border adjustment led to the US agreeing to a joint protection concept against "dirty" steel imports, and in many other areas such as hazardous waste, emission standards, animal testing, plant protection, antitrust and competition law (Bradford 2020). Even China had to bow to such regulations in recent years. This is not least due to the fact that the country, despite the size of its market, unlike the EU, cannot sell its products produced exclusively for the Chinese market everywhere in the world due to lower standards and norms. And it has something to do with the fact that European regulatory authorities are above any suspicion of corruption and their regulations for industry and consumers cannot be circumvented, in other words, they are less flexible than rules in the financial sector.

Most recently, the EU set out to develop rules for AI with the "Artificial Intelligence Act" ("AI Act"), particularly targeting companies that pose the greatest application risks. In this context, particularly problematic users, such as those who, like *Social Scoring* from China, force their own population into system-conforming behavior or conduct biometric surveillance, are banned, while all other applications are subject to minimal requirements at most.

The concern about one-sided dependencies on Russia (energy) or China (where economic dependencies actually exist in various product categories due to China's monopoly position) can thus be countered to some extent from the European side. However, the EU must be careful not to harm itself with its regulatory zeal by issuing regulations where it is not responsible, or prescribing testing procedures and proofs where the bureaucratic effort is out of proportion to the benefit. The tightrope walk consists in not allowing the high regulatory standards to become a location obstacle for investments and jobs and to impose comparatively higher prices on European consumers than elsewhere (Meyers 2023). The "Green Deal" adopted by the Commission with great effort is such a negative example, where Brussels' regulatory frenzy could ultimately harm its own economy. Among other things, it provides for the economy and the financial markets to become green in the future. If implemented, the subsequent taxonomy project, which classifies all investment decisions within the internal market as green or not green, is superfluous. Why almost 50,000 companies in Europe should be forced to submit further publications in the course of a so-called sustainability report, after they have been obliged for years to present their eco-balances, is known only to the Commission, but imposes unnecessary additional costs on medium-sized companies in particular. Nor is there a need for new uniform EU requirements for minimum wages or collective agreements, as long as social and labor market policy is largely a matter for the member states.

The AI Act is similarly critical. While the EU claims that 90% of applications would be exempt, it does not draw a clear line between dangerous and harmless AI. Industry stakeholders are already warning that the requirements could affect far more (50%), leading to additional bureaucracy and control costs. The message that follows from such warnings is well known. Despite all the justified complaints about the dangers of generative AI like ChatGPT, the EU once again runs the risk of hindering innovation by adhering to the precautionary principle in competition policy. At the same time, however, the US is promoting self-regulation, thereby boosting the innovative power of its own AI developers.

As long as Brussels' regulations do not come at the expense of economic growth and fair competition, the Union's potential as a global standard setter is considerable. Strict regulatory requirements in the environmental sector have certainly given green industries a head start within the Union. The lack of large tech companies in the EU is mainly due to the lack of venture capital and the slow progress in completing the internal market. This potential could be further enhanced by more consistent use of its own technological niche capacities and closer cooperation with the US.

The latter is also in Washington's interest. Although they are aware of Europe's dependence on their own country and China for future technologies such as cloud computing or artificial intelligence, they fear nothing more than China's growing influence on technological regulatory standards, as described above. Beijing supplies the corresponding technological infrastructure and AI-driven surveillance technology to illiberal recipient countries of the Silk Road Initiative worldwide, thereby undermining Western soft power. Washington would therefore equally benefit from close cooperation with the EU in regulating Big Tech and the digital economy. And it knows that, together with the EU, it can still bring about 40% of global GDP to bear to strengthen the "Brussels effect" towards a "green" transformation and digitization of the economy (Orszag 2023). This is also why previous disagreements between the two sides on issues of antitrust law, data protection, and taxation and subsidization of the necessary technologies are high on the agenda for the transatlantic Technology Council in Washington.

Another point comes into play: The US and Europe should strengthen their cooperation precisely because the now touted "de-risking" as a panacea for reducing dependencies, especially from China, in the sense of diversifying supply chains is correct, but by no means a guarantee for more stability and security. In Europe, the focus is particularly on the Southeast Asian markets to strengthen its own resilience. What sounds like a simple solution in theory is also fraught with uncertainties in practice. This is shown by a look at developments in the US. There, companies have started to shift their business towards the ASEAN states with some success since 2018. However, what initially appears positive in the balance sheets could not prevent trade between the ASEAN states and China from also expanding during the same period. The big winners of these trade shifts are therefore primarily the Southeast Asian countries, which can not only hedge on all sides and thus drive up the price, but have also become an important transshipment and transit region for Chinese goods heading to the US. In other words, despite statistical successes, the US has not become less dependent on China since then. Europe should be aware of the dangers of a possible division of the West in China's strategic interest in light of this experience. For Beijing, the ongoing economic dependence of Europe on China is the best insurance against possible EU sanctions.

Regardless of regulatory power and the need for cooperation with Washington to reduce dependencies in the digital economy, the EU remains an important market for both China and the US with its strengths in basic research and industrial application technologies. And as much as the Chinese sales market is of central importance for Europe, it remains limited for European companies overall. On average in the EU, the latter generated about 11% of their sales in China before COVID (2019) (Zenglein 2020). Especially in the area of investments and technological know-how, the EU remains one of the largest job creators alongside China and could, in turn, hit China hard with the introduction of the planned investment control to prevent takeovers of key technologies. The same applies to economic sanctions, the efficiency of which the Commission wants to increase through better knowledge of their targets and faster implementation (both in defending against sanctions and in counter-sanctions). On the way there, one must not be deterred, especially against the background of still strong market access restrictions, inadequate protection of intellectual property, and also the violation of human rights.

Restricted access to Chinese investments in the sense of reciprocity is also necessary because the EU and Germany have continuously expanded their trade shares with China in recent years, while China has successively reduced these in the sense of its "Two Circuits Strategy". However, this makes the EU and Germany relatively more dependent on China in the medium term and already today. Therefore, this dependence must be reduced, not in the sense of decoupling, but through diversification and the ability to overcome supply crises on global markets more flexibly (Brunnenmeier 2021)—by companies building up stocks like banks increasing their equity, through autonomous regional production chains to reduce the number of transports and CO_2 emissions where possible, through alternative supply routes, more investments in key technologies or the opening up of additional business partners. A distinction must be made between short-term necessary measures and long-term realistic goals. As ambitious as initiatives like the "EU Chips Act" with a funding volume of a total of 43 billion € may sound and as politically welcome as they may be, they are not feasible if they are not accompanied by pragmatic transitional solutions. The idea of bringing Europe back to the forefront of manufacturing state-of-the-art semiconductors by 2030 by promoting research and industrial use, better monitoring supply shortages in the future, intervening directly in production if necessary, attracting investments and expanding production in the EU, sounds good. However, given the lack of raw materials, dependence on imports, and high labor costs, the implementation of the project is fraught with great difficulties.

So what can Europe do? The obvious and simple answer would initially lie in the well-known demand for the enforcement of the majority principle in all matters of foreign economic policy and, associated with this, a deeper economic and financial integration, i.e., an expansion of the EU budget towards a European industrial policy. While the latter is probably associated with the greatest political obstacles, the Europeanization of foreign economic policy is gradually gaining momentum. Although trade policy is one of the areas that have been communitized in the EU, i.e., those in which qualified majority decisions are fundamentally possible, trade issues of security policy relevance still fall within the competence of the member states. However, such a national reservation right is no longer sustainable in times of global geo-economic power struggles. And even in the case of correct individual state decisions, it cannot develop nearly the impact that EU decisions can.

The export restrictions on technology for the production of computer chips imposed by the Netherlands at the beginning of 2023 were indeed based on the EU regulation on the export control of "dual use goods" (2021) with the aim of preventing military use and protecting the Netherlands' position in such technologies. The company most affected by the restrictions was ASML, based in the Netherlands. The largest semiconductor technology company in Europe produces so-called lithography machines, which are the basis of any chip production. The problem, however, is that the EU regulation places a very narrow focus on dual-use goods, as it is primarily tailored to preventing the proliferation of weapons. This significantly limits the EU's ability to effectively restrict trade in technologies in the semiconductor industry, "clean energy", biotechnology or robotics, which do not fall under this category but are of crucial importance for the EU's economic security. Only with appropriate creativity and an extensive interpretation of the EU regulation were the

Netherlands finally able to implement their own export restrictions—which does not rule out that the case may end up at the WTO. Much more decisive, however, is that the Dutch solo effort alongside the US can lose its effect at any time due to the decisions of other member states. If, for example, Germany continues to supply the optical and laser components necessary for the production of the Dutch machines from the companies Zeiss and Trumpf to China, the Dutch export restrictions would be at least significantly undermined and could thus destroy the potential European competitive advantage.

The EU as a whole now has control instruments in the field of critical technologies—such as the investment control agreement, export controls or protection agreements in international research cooperation. The example of the recently introduced instrument to counteract coercive measures by third countries (Anti-coercion instrument—ACI) points in the right direction: This regulation gives the EU as a block the opportunity to impose export controls in the case of such coercive measures—it is therefore in the best sense a strategic instrument that takes into account the security policy consequences of economic cooperation beyond purely economic and social results. Who will be ahead in the technology competition in the future is primarily a question of security policy relevance, and this is how it should be treated in Europe. In this sense, the establishment of an EU control instrument or committee for all security-relevant technologies, which ensures better coordination of national security interests with EU economic policy and ideally also allows the imposition of export restrictions, would be a step away from the hitherto reactive character of European foreign economic policy towards a more proactive geo-economic role of the EU on the global markets (Gehrke and Ringhoff 2023). This certainly has its price. But only in this way will Chinese countermeasures such as the recent export restrictions on gallium, geranium and graphite as important chemical elements for the production of semiconductors also become a higher risk for Beijing.

The EU has another lever through the targeted use of its niche potential where third countries are themselves in a dependency relationship with the Union. Europe does not have technology leadership in the areas central to the digital economy. It does not have the skills or resources to control the production cycle of entire sectors and any ambition in this direction would undoubtedly lead to a further escalation of the global subsidy race at a time when the EU's fiscal resources are already exhausted by prioritizing climate change and rebuilding Ukraine. Therefore, if the EU wants to increase its geo-economic influence, it must secure its leadership position at least in the specific technology segments that are central to the world economy's main supply chains. In this way, its own vulnerability and dependency can be at least partially mitigated and a certain deterrent capability against coercive measures by third parties can be developed.

In the field of critical raw materials, for example, the EU plays a central role in the development of technologies for their extraction, processing, and recycling. Europe provides companies with the most modern extraction and recycling equipment, thus having the technology providers that are central to this industry. And as much as the European standard for supply chain responsibility imposes additional burdens on companies in the short term, the irreversible trend towards more sustainable supply chains could provide them with competitive advantages through technology leadership in the medium term. More and more companies therefore see supply chain responsibility not only as a cost factor, but also as a strategic opportunity to gain a competitive advantage, establish closer connections with suppliers, and secure the supply of raw materials and intermediate products. In the field of quantum technology, the Union has significant competitive advantages in the application in the form of special lenses, and lasers, adhesives, cooling systems, or single-photon detectors. In the semiconductor sector, the Dutch corporation ASML and the German companies Zeiss and Trumpf could, as mentioned, form the spearheads of a generally more significant role of the EU in this technology field. The telecommunications providers Nokia and Ericsson, alongside Huawei, are among the world market leaders in the field of 5G networks, but will probably have to defend their position in the medium term against competitors when additional and open interfaces for competitors emerge as part of the "Open Ran" technology concept. Finally, in the case of China, there is still a great dependence on Europe for industrial machines, tools for chemical and physical analysis, and even militarily relevant elements in the space industry.

The greatest potential for Europe in the geo-economic competition with China and the US undoubtedly lies in the field of green technologies. Even though there is a great concern about a subsidy race with the two superpowers, Europe's export share (23% in 2022) of "green" goods is already considerable—albeit smaller than China's (34%), but definitely larger than that of the US partner (13%), whose catch-up process only began under the Biden administration. The own dependence on the six essential products of the green change (electric cars, batteries, heat pumps, solar panels, wind turbines, and electrolyzers) varies.

China is the undisputed world market leader in the extraction and processing of critical raw materials, which are necessary for the production of batteries, wind turbines, and solar panels. It mines about 70% of the global natural graphite and 66% of the rare earth elements, controls a dense network of mineral supply contracts with countries in South and West Africa, Oceania, and Latin America, which supplies its own recycling industry, dominates with a global market share of 85% also in the processing of rare earths and is also among the world market leaders in the processing of silicon and cobalt. This ensures the country an undisputed monopoly position with regard to EU imports of batteries (82%), wind turbines (90% for the necessary permanent magnets in production) and solar panels (90%) (Garcia-Herrero et al. 2023). This cannot be compensated overnight, regardless of how ambitious the Commission's plans may be. However, it can at least be cushioned by using one's own comparative advantages over China, for example in low-emission green goods. A number of European member states do indeed have such advantages, among them the Central European ones, Denmark, and also Germany with the highest export share in global comparison. If Europe bundles its potentials not least also through the promotion by the EU budget, more consistent exclusion of competitors from public tenders who do not comply with the rules of fair trade, and shorter approval times for European projects, it can compete on the global markets in the areas of decarbonization of industry, green technologies, and energy security and at least get within reach of the target of 40% of wind and solar plants, batteries, and heat pumps originating from domestic production by 2030 as envisaged in the "Net Zero Industry Act".

The advantage that the associated trend towards local production chains brings in the medium term also lies in the increasing importance of large distances for trade. As markets mature, production processes become more efficient, innovations produce cheaper and more effective products, and prices and margins decrease, technological quality differences between competitors will decrease. The result is that every cent of efficiency gain that manufacturers record is crucial, and as the transport of heavy goods such as electric vehicles and batteries becomes increasingly expensive due to high energy costs, the trend towards regional production also increases (Springford and Tordoir 2023).

Location and comparative advantages, such as in the field of electric vehicles, or where the Chinese and American markets are less open to European products than vice versa, must therefore also be defended with appropriate countermeasures. This is particularly true where Europe's stereotypical threat of anti-dumping and anti-subsidy proceedings before the WTO falls flat. Strong signals for the value of multilateral rules to global partners have been fizzling out for almost two decades now; and since then, the WTO's Doha Round of world trade has also been at a standstill. China spends just under 2% of its GDP on targeted industrial policy. The support measures range from direct subsidies and tax breaks to discounted land and loans to subsidies for commercial promotion. In addition, the state, with its large purchases, is the most important customer of many Chinese companies. In such an uncooperative global competition on the world markets, it is impossible to avoid subsidizing one's own industries. However, this must focus on areas where excessive dependencies exist or where hard security risks are identified, must not be done on a scattergun basis and must be temporary. A recent example is the market for wind turbines. On it, enormous scale effects can be achieved, similar to civil aviation. Airbus and Boeing dominate the latter globally, and America and Europe have long been in a massive subsidy competition. And such subsidies must be time-limited to flow into sectors where it is about the so-called start-up financing of companies. The uncertainties associated with supplying Europe with green hydrogen prevent private investments and therefore require incentives through publicly initiated projects. China supported European research and development in sectors such as photovoltaics and vehicles by encouraging EU companies to invest in production facilities in China and use joint ventures to gain technological know-how. In this context, the control and possible restriction of direct investments is a long overdue measure to protect the European economy.

"Global Gateway", Transatlantic Trade and the Search for Strategic Partners

The dependence on the raw material superpower China can otherwise be limited primarily by expanding or diversifying the EU's trade partnerships (Alcidi and Kiss-Galfalvi 2023). Both are fraught with costs and risks, but are essential both in terms of trade in goods and services and direct investments. However, if the Commission's ambitious goals are to be achieved, namely to be dependent on no country for more than 65% of the supply of strategically important raw materials, to cover at least 10% of the annual demand in Europe by 2030 and to process and refine 40% of this in the EU, it cannot afford and must not give in to the moods of those who recommend the Union to trade in the future only with friendly states "guided by values". Such an attitude would be fatal and counterproductive for a comparatively energy and raw material poor continent, which for climate policy reasons has not even thought about reducing dependencies through its own resource extraction for decades. As correct as it is to more consistently consider the geopolitical dimension of a supply chain policy hitherto focused on operational security. A change of course in the sense of the radical exclusion of illiberal systems may seem politically understandable, but is economically negligent, as it is associated with high financial costs and a considerable lead time. Where possible, companies should be left to decide how they ultimately design their supply chains based on their own risk assessments. For the US too, Biden's proposal of a global alliance of democracies did not mean that Washington can afford to choose its trading partners only among "like-minded" people. Even before Trump's return estimates already suggested a possible shift in the volume of 25% of global supply and commodity flows, the costs of which amounted to over 4 trillion dollars annually (Maihold 2022). Whether such a shift brings the hoped-for greater security can be doubted either way. Rather, a renewed global competition for low labor costs, suitable production and transport infrastructures and tax incentives is to be expected, especially between Europe and the US. It is already becoming apparent that both sides in the struggle for lower interdependence vulnerabilities and "more reliable" trading partners are looking at the same countries: Australia, Indonesia, Malaysia and Vietnam in the Indo-Pacific region, Canada and Mexico in the Americas, Romania and Bulgaria as well as the Mediterranean states in Europe. Whether Trump's disruptive trade policy with some of these target countries, particularly partners such as Canada and Mexico, gives Europe a better starting position, remains to be seen.

More pragmatism in diversifying trade partners therefore means from the EU's perspective, finding partners with compatible incentives, i.e., those who have a mutual interest in restructuring their economies towards greater integration into green supply chains—certainly a more favourable option for Brussels than "reshoring". And a mutually beneficial option, as long as Europe ensures that its own aid money is not used in many over-indebted countries to complete the projects of the "Silk Road Initiative" that are in financial difficulties. Countries with large deposits of critical raw materials such as Congo, Zambia or Namibia can in this way reduce their own dependence on just one or a few buyers and thus strengthen their negotiating position in the markets, while at the same time rising in the value chain of "Clean-Tech" production. China, itself the world's largest producer and supplier of critical raw materials, is nevertheless the largest buyer of rare earths from Namibia and also illegally mines them there through its own companies—with the aim of expanding its own monopoly position at a global level. To reduce such dependencies, Europe's "Global Gateway Initiative" wants to create alternative transport corridors to China's Silk Road project, to help recipient countries bring their raw materials to the world market; the planned "India-Middle East-Europe Economic Corridor" (IMEC), which is to supplement the trade between India and Europe previously handled via the sea route (Suez Canal) with new routes via Greece and Israel, is a first concrete project with which Europe wants to step out of China's geopolitical shadow. In addition, Europe can help these countries play a larger role in the refining and production of such raw materials. Especially for advanced industrial countries like Australia and Canada, which have corresponding own resources, this would offer the opportunity to thus secure a complementary supply chain advantage over China's demand monopoly in this area. Countries that, like India, Mexico or Turkey, have fewer resources but plenty of cost-effective production capacities, would in turn gain better access to both raw materials and markets for finished goods and could in the medium term become important strategic partners of Europe in the bundling of intellectual property (patent development) for the production of clean technologies.

Europe, due to its resource scarcity, must have an interest in such an upgrading of alternative raw material suppliers to China, in order to counteract the excessive concentration of the processing of critical raw materials in China at least to some extent. It is not able to mobilise large subsidy packages in the short term to protect its own economy, as long as the provision of such funds is a matter for the member states. Countries like Germany have other fiscal options than some highly indebted smaller member states in the EU. The internal market remains fragmented as long as these imbalances do not change and there is a lack of political will for a common fiscal union, which cannot function without financial compensation from the rich to the poorer member states or common macroeconomic order ideas. From an overall perspective, possible cost disadvantages, such as those brought about by the diversification of partnerships and supply chains, seem acceptable, especially if they also attract additional private investments in comparatively stable partner countries. In this way, one continues to rely on free and fair trade, whether with like-minded people, illiberal democracies or those countries that stand between the blocs or instrumentalise them in the sense of a targeted hedging policy (e.g. India, Turkey), but at the same time becomes more resilient to sanctions that Beijing, Washington or others impose on Europe in order to enforce their own geopolitical and economic goals.

Resilience also means the targeted use of countermeasures. The examination of Chinese direct investments for compatibility with national security interests or the "Instrument against Coercive Measures" planned by the EU are necessary steps in the competition with global system changers. As long as China wants to secure comprehensive intervention possibilities for the access of European companies, as long as it bans or restricts

4 The Geoeconomic Maps of the Future

foreign investments in entire sectors via so-called negative lists, Europe must in turn also be able to protect its own companies. This is not about preventing takeovers through prohibitions or upper limits for investment guarantees for German investments in China. It is about allowing German companies to participate in technological development by Chinese investors in accordance with the WTO principles of a general prohibition of discrimination, most-favoured-nation treatment and national treatment.

After all, these principles essentially provide a guarantee of minimum legal standards in dealing with foreign investors under international law, which every comprehensive investment agreement should contain. Investments abroad to build production and distribution structures always involve a business risk, as they are associated with high initial costs. Investment decisions therefore need separate guarantees in international agreements in order not to have to rely on the law and the courts of the host state for protection against overreaching state measures during this time.

Such determination Europe must also show in its future dealings with the US. A trade agreement with the US has now become a long way off no matter how beneficial it would be for both sides. It goes without saying that both sides are still closer to each other than in their respective relations with China. And of course, both Europe and Germany must make it clear that maintaining a policy of equidistance in the strategic relationship with China and the US is not an option against the backdrop of the emerging Moscow-Beijing axis and Beijing's subversion of Western democracies (Hamilton and Ohlberg 2022).

For Europe, this does not mean blind allegiance, as France recently rightly reminded political Berlin in the question of security policy cooperation. Already the first Trump years showed how quickly an ally can become a determined defender of its own geoeconomic interests. Biden also supported trade barriers to prevent the bleeding out of American industry, even if they were only of an indirect nature. Anyone who entices buyers of electric cars with tax credits if they were assembled 80% in America, or wants to mine 80% of the rare earths needed for drive batteries in the US in the future, is also shielding his economy at the expense of allies in Europe. With the recently adopted "Inflation Reduction Act" (IRA), Washington has also intensified competition by attracting foreign investors in climate-friendly technologies with subsidies that reduce production costs in the US by 30 to 40%.

While this is not open protectionism and should not be condemned as such in view of three-digit billion-dollar support programs in Germany and France, the EU is pursuing its own projects that are also directed against the US, such as the carbon tariff, which is intended to make imports of CO_2-intensive products more expensive. The problem with such subsidies is merely that they are much more bureaucratically designed and therefore do not take effect as quickly as tax credits, which Washington has been granting through the IRA since 2023. But even in relation to the US, Europeans should resist more strongly the state aid to support mainly domestic manufacturers, by insisting at least on equal treatment of European companies compared to US free trade partners like Canada and Mexico (Braml 2022).

Otherwise no one in Europe can have an interest in an escalation with Washington, even under Trump. Already during his first presidency, the close economic ties were in clear contrast to the political alienation between the two sides. Europe remains dependent on the US as its most important trading partner and needs Washington on its side in conflicts with China and Russia. However, this should not prevent Europe from exploiting the potential of its internal market vis-à-vis Washington, where it distorts competition, such as through the IRA or the export ban on high-tech chips, and puts European providers under pressure. In case of an intensified trade conflict with China it is likely that in the end Trump will orientate himself towards Europe again. Against the background of the system conflict with China and Russia and Beijing's increasing decoupling from the US trade may increase again with Europe. As a matter of fact, transatlantic trade has intensified in recent years (also under the first Trump presidency in the end), which particularly benefited US exports.

However, to compete in the geoeconomic competition with the US, a different signal from Brussels would be much more decisive: the completion of integration in the areas of banking and capital market union and the advancement of the fiscal union and the development of the digital Euro. The US mainly uses the strength of the leading world reserve currency, the dollar, to enforce geoeconomic interests. A public-law European bank alongside the European Investment Bank, which is not dependent on the dollar, would be a step to possibly deter the US from disrupting trade. Digital currencies with the corresponding European infrastructure and two different payment systems could also reduce dependence on the US financial system. How much the world, and thus Europe, is still dependent on the dollar, was painfully experienced by Europeans when Instex, an instrument of several EU countries to enable legal trade with Iran, failed miserably due to US resistance. Under the threat of secondary sanctions, most European companies shied away from further trade with Iran (Gehrke 2022).

In this context, the reduction of such dependency is urgently necessary against the backdrop of geo-economic power shifts. The theory of geo-economics is simple: it states that politics usually follows shifts in economic interests. The Euro-Atlantic area has grown together through mutual economic dependencies and has lost its overriding importance for the world economy in the age of globalization. This trend also has implications for the political cohesion of the community. For the US, the Indo-Pacific region has become the central geostrategic target region in the power struggle with China, and Trump has made it clear that Washington will buy the political loyalty of its allies through economic pressure if in doubt. For Great Britain, the vision of "global Britain" means an institutional departure from the European integration project. And in Germany too, the increasing economic weight shift towards the East (especially China) since the global financial crisis, despite all of Europe's dominance as the most important sales market, has had a significant influence on Berlin's (foreign) political decisions in recent years (Kundnani 2020). Even though the discussion about the growing importance of geo-economics, as indicated above, is primarily focused on its application by autocratic states like China or Russia and is often referred to as economic nationalism (instead of economic liberalism) in this context. With Trump's return, the US is now moving in same fairway. And states like Germany also use economic instruments for strategic purposes: whether through sanctions against third countries or interest rate fluctuations as a means of pressure against members of the Eurozone during the Euro crisis—such instruments always represent forms of a "liberal geo-economics" (Kundnani).

Against this backdrop, the Union will also have to assert its geo-economic power more strongly towards the

Eurasian mega-region in the future. Strategic key industries of the member states have, through their cooperation with China (5G technology), on the one hand, significantly challenged American leadership in the fourth industrial revolution, but on the other hand, they are technologically and security-politically vulnerable. States like Serbia or Turkey endanger the political cohesion of the Euro-Atlantic community through their cooperation with Russia and China. New transport corridors connect the Eurasian continent, thereby reducing the importance of controlling the most important geostrategic chokepoints by the US. Greece, Poland, Italy, Austria, Luxembourg, and Switzerland have joined the Chinese Silk Road initiative, thus creating the connection of the Eurasian sea and land routes. And the harmonization of the Russian Northern Sea Route with China's polar Silk Road to develop an Arctic transport corridor also creates economic opportunities and challenges for Europe (Diesen 2021).

To meet them, Europe will have to throw its full economic weight into the balance. However, it must also ensure that it remains committed to reciprocally offsetting disadvantages for its own companies in all countermeasures. The loss of market shares can indeed be calculated. This is the only way to defend free and fair trade—in all directions. And this is the only way the EU has a good chance of surviving in the global geo-economic power struggle and closing the gap to the US and China. This may be easier if one does not indulge in the illusion that the EU is a paragon of trade policy. And if critics of security-politically well-founded limitations of free economic activity did not always immediately interpret such as evidence of a moralizing foreign trade policy. Market shares are fought for on global markets. All market participants are subject to the eternal dilemma that they want to take advantage of the benefits of free trade and direct investments, but at the same time want to protect their political autonomy, cultural values, and social structures. The EU also uses non-tariff trade barriers in particular, thereby complicating global trade. For years, the most prominent example has been the subsidies and import restrictions in the EU agricultural sector, with which the EU not only burdens its own budget but also contributes to market distortions. More than half of all protectionist measures imposed worldwide come from the EU. And anti-dumping duties have long been a proven means of protecting against Chinese competition.

References

Alcidi, Cinzia, Tamas Kiss-Galfalvi: Economic Integration during an Age of Geopolitical Instability, CEPS Explainer, Brussels (September 2023)

Bradford, Anu: The Brussels Effect. How the European Union rules the World, Oxford University Press 2020

Braml, Josef: Die transatlantische Illusion. Die neue Weltordnung und wie wir uns darin behaupten könne, Beck: München 2022

Brunnenmeier, Markus: Die resiliente Gesellschaft. Wie wir künftige Krisen besser meistern können, aufbau-Verlag 2021

Charan, Ram, Rita McGrath: The radical reshaping of Global Trade, in: Harvard Business Review (November 1, 2023)

Diesen, Glenn: Europe as the Western Peninsula of Greater Eurasia, in: Journal of Eurasian Studies, Vol. 12 (1), 2021, pp. 19–27

Einfuhr und Ausfuhr der EU. https://de.statista.com (2022)

European Commission: European Industrial Strategy (Brussels, May 5, 2021); European Commission, Critical Raw Materialsfor Strategic Technologies and Sectors in the EU – A Foresight Study (2020)

Evenett, Simon, Johannes Fritz: Brazen Unilateralism: The US-China Tariff War in Perspective. The 23rd GTA Report. London 2018. https://www.alexandria.unisg.ch/handle/20.500.14171/99896

Federal Register, Vol. 85, No. 246 (22. December 2020), Rules and Regulations, pp. 83416–32. https://www.govinfo.gov/content/pkg

Flach, Lisandra, Feodora Teti: Die Zukunft der EU-China-Handelspolitik: Herausforderungen angehen und eigenen Handelsinteressen selbstbewußt vertreten, Wirtschaftsdient, 2021, Heft 11. www.wirtschaftsdienst.eu

Flach, Lisandra, J. Gröschl, M. Steininger, F. Teti und A. Baur: Internationale Wertschöpfungsketten – Reformbedarf und Möglichkeiten, Ifo-Studie für die Konrad-Adenauer-Stiftung e. V. 2021

Garciá-Herrero, Alicia, Heather Grabbe, Axel Kaellenius: De-risking and de-carbonizing: a green tech partnership to reduce reliance on China, Bruegel Policy Brief 19/23 (October 2023)

Garcia-Herrero, Alicia: Chinese Economic Statecraft: What to expect in the next five years?, in: Johann Strobl, Heiko Borchert (eds.), Storms Ahead. The Future Geoeconomic World Order, Wien 2022

Gehrke, Tobias: EU open Strategic Autonomy and the Trappings of Geoeconomics, in: European Foreign Affairs Review 27, Special Issue (2022), pp. 61–78

Gehrke, Tobias, Julian Ringhof: Instrument of Control: How the EU can protect itself in the global technology competition, European Council on Foreign Relations (June 21, 2023)

Geinitz, Christian: Chinas Griff nach dem Westen, München 2022, p. 13 ff.

Hamilton, Clive, Mareike Ohlberg: Die lautlose Eroberung. Wie China westliche Demokratien unterwandert und die Welt neu ordnet, Pantheon: München 2022

Huang, Yukon: The US-Chinese Trade War has become a Cold War, Carnegie Endowment for International Peace (September 16, 2021)

Johnson, Luke: What Europe thinks …..About trade, Internationale Politik Quarterly, Berlin (January 2023). https://ip-quarterly.com/en

Kleine-Brockhoff, Thomas: Tauglicher Universalismus, in: Internationale Politik (September/Oktober 2023), pp. 106–109

Klingebiel, Stephan: Engagement mit Partnern im Globalen Süden in Zeiten von Unsicherheiten, German Institute of Development and Sustainability (IDOS), Policy Brief (2/2022)

Kroeber, Arthur: China's economy, Oxford 2020, p. 30 ff.

Kundnani, Hans: Germany's liberal geo-economics: using markets for strategic objectives, in: Wigell, Scholvin, Aaltola, Geo-Economics and Power Politics in the 21st. Century, London: Routledge 2020, pp. 61–74

Maihold, Günther: Die neue Geopolitik der Lieferketten. Friend-Shoring als Zielvorgabe für den Umbau von Lieferketten, SWP-Aktuell A 45 (21. Juli 2022)

Matthes, Jürgen: Gegenseitige Abhängigkeit im Handel zwischen China, der EU und Deutschland, Institut der Deutschen Wirtschaft, Köln /IW-Report 35/2022

Meyers, Zach: In Tech, the death of the Brussels Effect is greatly exaggerated, Center for European Reforms, Brussels (December 8, 2023)

Mold, Andrew: Why South-South trade is already greater than North-North trade, Brookings Commentary (December 11, 2023), Washington

Oermann, Nils Ole, Hans-Jürgen Wolff: Wirtschaftskriege. Geschichte und Gegenwart, Freiburg/Basel/Wien: Herder 2023, p. 147

Orszag, Peter: Do not underestimate the „mega Brussels effect" of EU-US coordination, Financial Times (October 16, 2023)

Pisani-Ferry, Jean: The Geopolitical Conquest of Economics, Project Syndicate 2021. www.theglobaleye.it

Plagemann, Johannes, Henrik Maihack: Wir sind nicht alle. Der Globale Süden und die Ignoranz des Westens, München: Beck-Verlag 2023, p. 192

Posen, Adam: The End of China's Economic Miracle. How Beijing's struggles could be an opportunity for Washington, in: Foreign Affairs (August 2, 2023)

Rudd, Kevin: Avoidable War, New York: Public Affairs 2022, p. 34 ff.

Siripurapu, Anshuh, Noah Berman: The Contentious US-Chinese Trade Relationship, Council on Foreign Relations: Backgrounder (September 26, 2023)

Springford, John, Sander Tordoir: Europe can withstand American and Chinese subsidies for green tech, Centre for European Reform, Brussels (June 2023)

Zenglein, Max: Mapping and recalibrating Europe's economic interdependence with Mercator Institute for China Studies (MERICS), 18. November 2020

5

Germany's Previous Economic Model Under Scrutiny

Like no other country in Europe, Germany has lived in recent decades on the idea that trade prevents war, and that foreign economic policy is primarily conducted under commercial auspices. "Change through trade" was the mantra in German foreign economic policy, at least as popular as the belief in the "culture of restraint" in foreign and security policy, as German politics across party lines nurtured for decades. Entrepreneurial interests were considered to coincide with the national interests of the country, but foreign economic and security policy issues were separated. For a country with an export share of over 50% of gross domestic product, this is not surprising. Germany's prosperity was and remains highly dependent on open markets. The country is proud of its export tradition, but sometimes also blind to alternatives. This is also why, with an openness rate of more than 85%, it is the most open economy among the leading industrial nations. Almost 30% of German jobs depend directly or indirectly on exports, in the manufacturing sector the number is even 55%. This is complemented by direct and indirect direct investments amounting to almost 1500 billion euros in the past two years.

However, export surpluses are not inherently good. They are indeed an expression of a capable economy or industry, especially if it is possible to achieve sufficient prices for the products sold on the world markets; both components cover the so-called "terms of trade", which indicate how many units of an imported product the economy receives for one unit of its export product. But they can also be a sign of a lack of societal distribution of profits, if it remains with export-strong companies or their owners or the majority is invested or deposited abroad (capital export) (Hesse 2023). It is now becoming clear how this strategy has led to years of neglect of necessary investments (infrastructure, digitization, education). This development was further promoted by the state's promotion of direct investments abroad with tax money. But there is also this: What is a guarantee of growth for the country and the basis of its prosperity model, makes it highly vulnerable from a geoeconomic perspective and severely restricts foreign policy options. In the case of Russian energy supply the country has now painfully experienced how quickly strategic partnerships can turn into one-sided dependencies. Russia's war in Ukraine and the associated gas supply shortages caught German politicians and entrepreneurs unprepared. The anxious question now is whether the overall stronger integration of China into the world economy can prevent the West as a whole, and especially Germany, from possibly facing a similar fate in the course of Beijing's isolation policy and whether we are even sliding into deindustrialization with our eyes wide open, as some observers are already warning.

Such a scenario seems exaggerated and corresponds to the country's tendency to make hasty predictions of decline in times of crisis. Measured by industrial gross value added, Germany is still not doing so badly in international comparison. After all, the value is around 20%, significantly higher than the EU average of 16% or in France and the US with just 11%. Nevertheless, the medium-term economic outlook for structural reasons (infrastructure, lack of modernization of the state and administration, irrational energy policy, far too long geopolitical ignorance) is currently rather gloomy. Even if inflation decreased and real wages may increased in 2024, it remains questionable against this background whether corporate investments will increase again, even though German companies have accumulated astonishing efficiency reserves over years of boom. But it is certain that the country is facing a major transformation in which the world economy is determined by competition and resource scarcity, demographic change will only succeed through technologically-digital productivity advances as long as an immigration policy oriented towards the needs of the labor market does not take place, and in which the threatened return of inflation significantly restricts the scope of debt-financed expenditure policy. And it is also certain that the country believed for far too long that it could arrange itself with the big ones and neglect the small ones. Now the focus on Russia and China is proving to be a strategic mistake and Germany is desperately seeking strategic partners from Asia to the Near and Middle East, from Africa to Latin America.

Germany's economic future will crucially depend on a change of course, especially in its China policy. The ominous concentration of power in the hands of China's state and party leader Xi Jinping, his obsession with the supposed superiority of the Chinese system over the West, which for a long time made it difficult for the regime in Beijing to deviate from its zero-Covid strategy despite devastating economic consequences, bodes ill. Both together, and the demographic development of a misogynistic society, suggest that China's seemingly unstoppable rise to the largest economy within three decades has passed its peak. In 2023, the country even faced the threat of a recession for the first time. And for 2024 the OECD states growth of just 4.8%, which is far below China's historical growth rates of almost 8% per year achieved over many years. Youth unemployment has risen to 20% and the real estate market is facing one of the biggest crises of confidence since the country's economic rise. At the same time, such pressure on the economy increases the risk of a Chinese attack on Taiwan, as the leadership might be inclined to offset the impending loss of prosperity with nationalist propaganda. The modernization of the military and the wolf warrior diplomacy promoted by the leadership certainly suggest this.

For Germany and its industry, the emerging development represents a dramatic economic challenge and opportunity at the same time. In the first half of 2022, during the Ukraine war, German investments in China once again reached record levels. Germany imports more from no other country than from China, and in terms of exports, the country ranks second. Conversely, the share of Chinese goods exports to Germany in all of China's goods exports fell from around four to about three percent between 2010 and 2021. Overall, Germany is much more dependent on trade with China than vice versa, and this asymmetry has steadily increased.

Such dependence on an increasingly aggressive system competitor will persist even with a slowly growing economy for the foreseeable future and poses a high risk for

Germany. China controls 90% of the processing of the most important metals for the construction of electric cars and renewable energies, it is highly integrated into German supply chains and cares little about the protection of intellectual property. Even in the global competition for semiconductors, the heart of the digital world, from cars, smartphones, servers to medical technology, the country is at least in the area of manufacturing such chips with larger structural width (not in the so-called "cutting-edge" chips, i.e. the most modern high-performance chips!) leading worldwide and central for the supply of Europe, especially Germany, in the above-mentioned industrial sectors.

Despite all dependence, however, the increasing isolation and the country's relapse into totalitarian rule should actually make it easier for German politics and business to more consistently advance the divestment and diversification process (mind you, not decoupling!) from the Chinese market already initiated at the European level and to fundamentally rethink Germany's dependence on raw materials. After all, according to surveys, more than half of the German population now view dependence on China as critical and wish for a redirection of investments to other countries.

How this can happen is shown by a look at the examples of Japan and South Korea. There, since 2023, companies have been legally required to create supply plans for critical raw materials and components that demonstrably show a diversification of their supply sources and an increase in their inventory levels. Why not also bundle private and public funds in subsidies and loan guarantees here to promote the extraction, further processing and recycling of raw materials, to pool purchases like now with gas, to support companies? One should not rely on a similar development occurring in the case of sanctions against China as in Russia, where critical raw materials were deliberately kept out of the sanctions regime in mutual interest.

Xi will increasingly orient his country towards isolation and independence from Western markets in the future and is willing to pay a high price for this. The contempt he shows for the hitherto successful business models of the technology giants Alibaba, Tencent, Meituan or JD.Com is an indication of this. China is not only increasingly focusing on localization, "individual innovation" and the displacement of still tolerated modernization helpers from abroad. It is also increasing state control of private entrepreneurship, which now accounts for almost two thirds of the gross domestic product. How far the Chinese leadership will go in this respect is open. Optimists hope that after overcoming Covid, the country's economic policy will be relaxed and private companies will regain more flexibility, but one should not count on this. For Germany, it is therefore time to "conditionalize" its own foreign trade policy more strongly and to adapt it to the above-mentioned European strategic competition with China. The geopolitical reaction to Russia must be followed by the geo-economic response to China, as long as Beijing sticks to its current course. This too is part of the urgently needed change in mentality.

This adjustment process will be associated with greater losses of prosperity, as are all limitations of international division of labor. For an economy whose industrial value creation depends almost two-thirds on foreign demand and the import of important preliminary services, the current unwinding of globalization inevitably means high adjustment costs. The Ifo Institute calculates a comprehensive relocation of production with a ten percent decrease in gross domestic product. Anyone can imagine the social explosive force such a development harbors. Against the background of China's ambivalent attitude in the Ukraine question and the radical change of course in Beijing, however, greater strategic independence is inevitable and will pay off in the long term. As correct as it may have been for a long time that foreign trade formed the most important basis of German prosperity and enabled the country to utilize specialization advantages and efficiency gains. A country must at least partially forego such if these efficiency gains come at the expense of security and vulnerability to crises—be it through external shocks as in the case of the pandemic, be it through increasing protectionism by system competitors or declining demand. And it is obvious that countries with a high degree of specialization like Germany are particularly vulnerable to crises in such cases.

China rigorously uses its economic power as a political weapon and makes trade partners susceptible to blackmail. One cannot continue to respond to such a policy with offers of dialogue and the terse note that sanctions do not cause a change of direction, but stronger demarcation and nationalisms. It is about preserving the greatest possible degree of benefits through economic networking while at the same time limiting political-economic vulnerabilities. The latter naturally weigh heavily in the case of Germany as an export-oriented country focused on the manufacturing sector. In the recent past, this export dependence of its economy has drawn criticism from EU partner countries for exporting unemployment to their countries. Often overlooked in this criticism is the fact that 40% of Germany's exports consist of imported preliminary services mainly from EU partner states, thus contributing to their international competitiveness. Now this export dependence seems to be becoming the country's downfall. Higher inflation and global isolationist tendencies are particularly affecting the countries of the north in the EU, where logically the share of industry in GDP is falling, while it is rising again in other parts of the EU (south). However, Germany is not at risk of becoming the "sick man" of Europe again for this reason, and the main reason for its current weakness or vulnerability certainly does not lie solely in China, even if politicians and experts like the media suggest otherwise. The country must rather realistically assess its dependence on China and options for a strategic change.

Between Technology Security, Diversification, and Connectivity

The German economy today faces three major challenges: It must *firstly* prevent the further transfer of technical knowledge to *domestic* companies in autocratic systems associated with exports and direct investments. This is actually also in the interest of companies, but should at least not be facilitated by investment and export credit guarantees for individual companies and entire sectors, Hermes guarantees for foreign projects or even rescue by the taxpayer on the part of politics. Only in this way will the risks in the boardrooms be reconsidered in terms of higher premiums with insurance companies and banks. It must *secondly* facilitate domestic investments in cutting-edge technologies and critical infrastructure and prevent the settlement of unwelcome investors in Germany, as in the case of Huawei's advance into critical telephone infrastructure. Such examples make it clear how difficult politics still finds it today to weigh up short-term economic successes and long-term security policy and strategic requirements. And it must *thirdly* prevent the great dependence on important raw materials, which the country, unlike other industrialized countries, has secured mainly through purchases on the world market, but not through its own direct investments in the raw materials sector, through more diversification and connectivity.

It is obvious that the latter in particular is the Achilles heel in terms of Germany's economic security. Not without reason does the aforementioned EU "de-risking" strategy aim primarily at addressing China's dominance in parts of the green supply chain. A look at the dependencies in the semiconductor and microchip sector makes the dangers of the previous China policy clear. For far too long, business and politics here followed the motto "purchases before direct investments". Only the shock experiences of interrupted supply chains and supply shortages in the wake of the demand increase after the COVID recovery triggered overdue discussions about the increasing technology dependence of the German industry on a few Asian (especially Chinese) and American providers. Meanwhile, politics has been talking for years about the need for greater independence from China and other autocracies, but also the US, from renewable energies and in this context the necessity to be able to produce semiconductors and battery cells in the future. But what levers does one have especially against states like China, which deliberately create dependencies and vulnerabilities, if one does not let them feel their own dependencies in return?

The US has long decided to leverage its technological superiority through a targeted industrial and innovation strategy against China, using it as a weapon by restricting the export of highly sensitive semiconductor technology and high-performance chips usable for military purposes to China. Together with Japan and the Netherlands, two of the most important locations for chip machine manufacturers, they are doing exactly what Germany continues to find difficult: developing a strategic vision that cuts off China from one of the most important high-tech products from Western production. This is not about complete isolation or decoupling; maintaining China's partial dependencies in these areas is always the better strategy (Scharre 2023). It's about control over the areas that are crucial for one's own national security. Primarily affected are those chips of the latest technology generation that are relevant for military modernization, i.e., artificial intelligence in military technology and improved weapon control, but also for monitoring their own citizens. Chips used for computers, mobile phones, or cars are explicitly exempt from the export ban. In this way, Beijing is forced into a conflict of objectives between the development of its own semiconductor technology and the globalization goals of leading companies for the purpose of profit maximization.

This was also the thinking in Berlin for a long time: instead of investing in future technologies, the focus was on the expansion of globally operating companies. And in Berlin, people still prefer to think about how America's politics could affect their own country and whether they could be drawn into Washington's sanction regime against China, rather than defining with the EU which technologies should fall under export controls and the screening of foreign investments. Here too, the country finds the change of times very difficult. It vacillates between the EU's rather narrowly defined definition of security-relevant technology and a rather vague, broader conception of it, which in turn carries the risk of massively undermining trade. The rejection in 2022 by the Federal Ministry of Economics of four applications by the VW Group for the extension of investment guarantees is certainly a correct signal, but it misses the core of the problem. Especially since the rejection officially also occurred for "human rights reasons" to superficially fit into the image of a "value-led" foreign policy. However, this rejection is a signal to China and German companies: If VW, BASF, Siemens or Bosch base their investment decisions solely on sales opportunities (the VW Group operates around 40 plants with partners in China), then they alone bear the responsibility for this in the future. The abolition of investment guarantees represents a paradigm shift in politics, which is not driven solely by the fight for human rights, but also has solid economic interests of the country behind it.

Nevertheless, this decision is only a first step. And what is difficult for politics, has been dawning on large parts of the economy for a long time. Even before Corona, companies had started to rely more on European suppliers and regional production chains, for example to stop or reverse the crash of the European share of global semiconductor production from 30% (1990) to currently less than 10% (with a target size of 20% in 2030). Meanwhile, politics still operated on the principle of warning about China on the one hand, but supporting the investment decisions of large corporations on the other. But now companies are voluntarily distancing themselves from China and openly demanding nothing less than a stronger politicization of the industry, i.e., to consider security policy considerations in addition to profit maximization, according to the motto: Of course, the high unit numbers that VW sells mainly on the Chinese market also secure jobs in Germany, where a part of the development still takes place. But what if Xi makes good on his threat of annexing Taiwan and thus cuts off the world from the center of the global microchip industry? Then the car production in this country is threatened with collapse.

A dual strategy of politics and economy is therefore indispensable. Decoupling from China is not possible, but a partial relocation of investments after examining dependencies and unused potentials in the form of outsourcing to other countries or joint ventures is urgently necessary. One does not have to immediately lay the axe to the already limited world trade, but the geopolitical risks associated with China's course should not be downplayed. Equally naive is the view that the relocation of supply chains and diversification are available at no cost or that subsidies would change the long-term comparative cost advantages; a conversion of supply chains to local producers forces the division of the world economy into regional blocks and means immense costs for all involved. The IMF estimates the associated costs for global GDP at 7.5 trillion US$. What this means for one's own society has so far not been communicated to the citizens of the country.

The middle ground lies in initially protecting areas that carry special economic and security policy risks, clearly signaling to autocracies like China that violations of the rules of the world trade order will be punished by resorting to one's own considerable potential for countermeasures, and supporting investments in public goods to strengthen economic security at the European level. This is the only plausible response to adapt to the new great power rivalry for market shares and technological leadership. It is not about engaging in the system competition provoked primarily by China and Russia in the sense of a displacement competition in which everyone loses. It is also not about conveying to the other side the idea of westernizing the world; this attempt has miserably failed in the past two decades. It is about understanding system competition as an ongoing challenge, preserving one's own model and making it attractive to others.

Strategic priorities must therefore also be set in securing raw materials. The approximately 3 billion € in funding that Berlin has contributed to the European joint project IPCEI (Important Projects of Common European Interest) for this purpose is a first step to reduce dependence on scarce and expensive raw materials, but is far from sufficient for the ambitious environmental and climate policy goals. Companies have indeed begun to relocate production sites within Asia and to Europe and to redesign entire components for which they need less "risk material". They are building reserve capacities in case of failure of main suppliers, in order to be able to almost compensate the costs of regional production in the medium term by reducing transports and CO_2 emissions and bypassing possible trade restrictions. However, the ambition of this goal is also demonstrated by the example of car production. Experts estimate a 30% increase in the cost of European cars in the case of such relocations. The price for a European demand for microchips covered from the EU internal market and the production of necessary preliminary and intermediate products is immensely high. The new independence therefore requires uncomfortable decisions and more financial support for companies from exploration to approval to procurement and processing in Europe.

Prudent politicians are well aware of this, but have so far hesitated to act in this direction. For this reason, only 2% of all direct investments in the energy sector were made in recent years. There was no talk of a strategy to invest in deposits instead of buying raw materials. Only with the discussion about the importance of sourcing Russian nickel and cobalt for the "green" transformation of German industry in the course of the Ukraine war did the idea of stockpiling such strategic raw materials even get started. Germany was driving by sight and reacted as after the oil crisis in 1973, when Russia threatened with a delivery boycott of oil and gas. The law for a national gas reserve was initiated. It should not even come to this in the case of stockpiling critical raw materials, but it would if short-term boycotts from the Chinese side are to be expected. The country therefore urgently needs a stronger role for politics in securing raw materials, as is the case in the US, Japan or South Korea. There, the military or state agencies are responsible for raw material stockpiling in close consultation with industry, which makes the countries overall more crisis-resistant.

Such a paradigm shift must be flanked by securing important trade routes and hubs on land on the sea routes. This too is part of improving one's own resilience. Participation in European initiatives to combat piracy off the Horn of Africa or in the Indo-Pacific or the sale of military goods to affected countries is not enough. If one does not want to confront countries like China more robustly militarily, then greater resilience can only be achieved by at least preventing digital and technological blackmail. China has long secured an almost insurmountable lead in the digital processing of international trade (connectivity) through the very energy-intensive blockchain technology as part of the Silk Road Initiative, but at the same time is blocking its own technology transfer more than ever. The same threat exists in the area of exploration, use and control of space, which is closely linked to the country's military and cyber ambitions.

Chinese hacker attacks, like those in the case of Russia, are part of the daily business of companies and operators of critical infrastructure. This is not only about industrial espionage and theft of intellectual property, but also about manipulation of political information spaces (Huotari 2022). When, as in the Hamburg case of the acquisition of shares in the Tollerort terminal by the shipping company Cosco, Chinese companies position themselves in key markets and buy into critical land-based infrastructure, then the danger of selling out the entire virtual supply chain of services in trade to China is quite real. Cosco makes no secret of the fact that its corporate goals are oriented towards the interests of the CCP and the Chinese state. In the past, the company often initially participated as a minority company at strategically important points, before it then acquired more shares, as in the Greek port of Piraeus, and thus gained control. Since then, Piraeus has been systematically expanded as a transshipment point for Chinese goods in a catchment area that now extends beyond Southern Europe to Prague.

A New China Strategy

The main concern is therefore to prevent the obvious geopolitical expansionist drive of an autocratic country that, as a trading power conducting more than 90% of its trade by sea, naturally has an interest in controlling its trade routes. However, its primary aim is to reduce its own vulnerability to American sanctions and to prevent possible European participation in a sanctions regime by cutting them off from central logistics and transport hubs. The risk that the infrastructure would no longer be controllable by the federal government in the event of a conflict with China cannot be dismissed. Conversely, one searches in vain for reciprocal co-control of port infrastructure at terminals in Chinese ports through German participation. On the contrary, access to procurement and investments is further complicated by China's recent efforts to improve its own law enforcement. They practically force German and European institutions to disclose country-specific technology dependencies and entanglements and to fend them off not only within the framework of the Transatlantic Trade and Technology Council, but also with other partners such as Japan, Australia or Taiwan in the sense of "friend-shoring".

The consequences arising from these challenges for German trade and financial policy are therefore obvious. A geo-economic strategy for Germany must first bring the actual balance of power, dependencies and vulnerabilities in German foreign trade more into focus. In fact, Germany has for far too long accepted that China's industrial policy has increasingly put its own flagships under pressure through "joint venture" projects. The Chinese automotive industry is on the verge of overtaking the German industry not only in terms of volume, but also in terms of quality in the field of electromobility, just as the solar industry did a decade ago. Chinese niche companies are increasingly putting pressure on the German Mittelstand, not to mention the lead that the country has long since gained in the areas of AI, electromobility and digitization.

Nevertheless, there is a distorted image in the German public, to which politics and business have made a significant contribution through their years of kowtowing to China. Export dependencies on the two superpowers US and China are still often portrayed very one-sidedly, thus creating the impression of an overall too great vulnerability of the German economy. It is true that the EU also supports the tech industry from battery production to electric cars with considerable funds, and of course the rise of the tech industry in these areas in China is also a reflection of its increased competitiveness. But such arguments should not prompt either Brussels or Berlin to refrain from doing what countries like the US, India or Turkey have long been doing with their protective tariffs to counter China's undisputed subsidy practices. There is ample evidence that Beijing is violating WTO rules. And it is undisputed that China directly supports its companies and not, as in the case of Germany, indirectly through purchase incentives or tax benefits for consumers. Despite all the undisputed dependency, there is still a feeling in Germany that everything depends on China. However, even the exports of the large automotive and chemical industries account for less than 1% of German gross value added, and that of the machinery and electrical industry even less than 1%. The public image regarding dependencies on the Chinese market therefore does not correspond to the overall economic reality. And even if China does not need Germany as a sales market as much as vice versa, Germany is all the more important as a gateway to Europe. China exports more to the EU than vice versa and is therefore also more vulnerable to punitive tariffs.

Apart from that, the current development in China is also often overestimated. The results of China's spending policy to support its state-owned enterprises are at best mixed, since the government has been pursuing active industrial policy (Posen 2023b). In any case, they have not demonstrably increased the productivity of Chinese companies. The best example is the semiconductor industry, where nearly 2 billion in state aid has not led to the sector catching up with the world's leading companies. If it looks like it does in the solar industry and in electromobility, then there are other reasons. Following the motto "more helps more", subsidies have given both industries an additional boost despite already generous profits, leading to European and American competitors losing market share. This makes it clear that politics should take a close look at where and to what extent subsidies flow, when investments actually have a chance of catching up with or even making up for technological backwardness, and when they promise start-up advantages on the global markets at approximately the same international level of development. All of this requires market expertise, where subsidies create overall economic and not just sector-specific competitive advantages, or where they merely lead to a redistribution between sectors and investments in better location conditions are ultimately the more promising solution.

Today, Germany conducts about two-thirds of its trade with the EU-27 and the United Kingdom. In contrast, only 2.7% of our gross domestic product depends on Chinese final demand, similar to the share of the US in German GDP (both combined account for just under 6%!). The problem is primarily the strong concentration on our large-scale industry (about a third of their turnover is generated by the automotive, chemical, pharmaceutical industry in China), while overall, China weighs much less economically than is generally assumed. Moreover, China's share of German value creation has remained at a relatively constant level in recent years. The Bundesbank also points to the comparatively small share of China in the total turnover of foreign subsidiaries of German companies of just under 8% (just under 200 billion out of a total of 2.4 trillion €!).

Much more decisive, however, is that the mutual dependencies are stronger than they are often portrayed. The costs of a complete economic decoupling from China are certainly considerable, but they are manageable, as the Institute for the World Economy (IfW) in Kiel recently calculated. In the case of Germany, it would amount to about 5% of gross national expenditure in the short term—a value that corresponds approximately to the slump in the German economy in the first year of the Covid pandemic. In the medium to long term, however, the loss would be much lower (1.5%), as German companies would naturally reorient themselves primarily towards the western economic bloc (IfW 2023); according to surveys by the Munich-based Ifo Institute, about 75% of German companies are currently working to diversify their supply chains. But what is more interesting is what the IfW notes with regard to China: the costs of decoupling are relative to economic power, similar to Russia, both short and long term higher than for any other western country, in the case of Germany about 60%!

If China wants to secure its rising prosperity, orientation towards Germany is indispensable. Both sides supply each other in the areas of electrical machines, apparatus and devices, with China obtaining high-quality technology especially in measuring and testing instruments, aircraft and spacecraft, as well as pharmaceuticals. However, China's dependence is particularly significant when considering the advantages of Germany's integration into the European internal market and the Euro. Otherwise, Germany does not play an outstanding role as a supplier and sales market from a Chinese perspective.

China is still more dependent on the EU as its most important supplier and second most important sales market than vice versa (at least in terms of gross exports) and is therefore not really interested in a larger trade conflict with Germany—especially against the backdrop of the escalating trade dispute with the US under Trump. A decoupling from both markets, i.e. from the West as a whole, is something the country currently has to fear at least as much as Germany fears the decoupling from Russian energy supplies and the Chinese market. On the other hand, the dependence on European exports to the US is still greater than vice versa.

Europe as a lever, the US as an ally

The first central premise of German foreign trade policy must therefore be the consistent strengthening of a geo-economically capable EU, as outlined in the previous chapter. The internal market is also Germany's most reliable lever when it comes to persuading trade partners to behave in a nearly rule-compliant and reciprocal manner. And as long as the principle of unanimity in questions of energy security or European sanctions policy delays or even prevents the implementation of geo-economic instruments, it is all the more urgent that Germany not only ostensibly advocates institutional reforms, but above all takes significant financial resources in hand to support the EU as a whole in enforcing geo-economic interests. With its financial weight, Germany can make a decisive contribution to shaping European trade and industrial policy. Hesitation, as in the case of the reaction to arms deliveries, or solo efforts, as in the case of an oil and/or gas embargo and a European gas price cap, therefore undermine urgently needed European solidarity and ability to act and won't work in the future. No affirmations help, even if one contributes about a quarter of the EU budget. At the same time, the double (security policy and economic) dependence on the US, which is the second premise of German foreign trade policy, should leave no doubt about whose side Germany is on in the geo-economic power struggle between China and the US as long as Trump doesn't give up on the European sales markets completely, which are still not replaceable. As long as this doesn't happen one should by no means hope for a return of times when one could comfortably pursue a policy of equidistance between both economic blocs in Berlin (Jäger 2022).

In questions of access to and control over important resources and intermediate products, the securing of trade routes and the influence on the stability of economically important partners, Germany will not be able to reduce its dependencies and vulnerabilities in the short term. For far too long, the country has chronically underestimated the proportion of critical raw materials in the overall impressive import volume. At best, statistics in the past were limited to checking or documenting the replaceability of such raw materials. Therefore, the greatest challenge for Germany and Europe lies in the diversification of the procurement countries of raw materials. And it is much harder to organize than for end products, where free trade agreements with emerging and developing countries offer the best chance to support companies in diversifying their supply chains.

Indeed, the country quickly responded to its unilateral energy dependence on Russia. However, it is surprising that it took such a shocking experience before Germany seriously started looking for European partners in the Mediterranean, especially considering its exit from coal and nuclear power. From an ideological perspective, nothing would have been more obvious. Given that Germany has been transforming its economy towards decarbonization for more than a decade, it would have been at least consistent to meet the demand for green electricity earlier where the best conditions for it exist. But only now does it seem to dawn on political Berlin that its own capacities in wind and solar energy are probably not sufficient and that the Mediterranean region, consisting of EU and non-EU countries, can provide the necessary capacities. This also applies to the Mediterranean access to the liquefied gas supply, which offers alongside what the US provides limited alternatives to Russian gas in the short term.

Regardless, Germany's perspective on raw material dependencies must become more global. Securing the most important trade routes is essential for supplying the German economy with raw materials from the Indo-Pacific. This requires not only a greater contribution in terms of military engagement to counter China's aggressive behavior in the region, but also the expansion of strategic raw material partnerships beyond China. Germany maintains various cooperations with resource-rich countries such as Chile, Peru, or Mongolia. However, geopolitical changes in the Indo-Pacific force Berlin to further diversify.

With the Indo-Pacific concept, which replaces the construct of the East Asian-Pacific area that has dominated for more than three decades as the geopolitical frame of reference for numerous countries, the strategic cards in the large region are being reshuffled. Above all, the US, Australia, India, and Japan determine the affiliation to the region, its power centers, and the thematic foundations of regional cooperation. It is not to be overlooked that security policy challenges dominate: the Indo-Pacific is perceived as an increasingly contested maritime area, which China is imprinting its stamp on by building artificial, militarily used islands in the South China Sea, modernizing its navy, and making blatant threats to other neighboring countries. In this new constellation, there is little room for European and German ideas of multilateral forms of cooperation. Instead, bi- and plurilateral, flexible partnerships such as Quad and AUKUS prevail. If one refuses them, one risks the criticism of precisely those countries that one needs (especially India and Australia), but only half-heartedly addresses their strategic challenges posed by China.

The fact that the changes in the Indo-Pacific are rather presented as a zero-sum game, in which strategic partners of the region and NATO allies side with the US, therefore meets the expectations of the US. And it is obvious that this is linked to the political signal that America's commitment in Europe can only be considered secure in the case of support in the region. The times when America's almost unconditional support for Europe was considered in its own geostrategic interest are over. Meanwhile, the pressure on Germany is also increasing because those countries that Berlin would like to have as strategic partners in the global power struggle with Russia and China alongside Europe in the expansion of the G7 states to G10 have clearly positioned themselves. The best example of this is the so-called

AUKUS alliance between the US, Great Britain, and Australia; in the medium term, Australian submarines will be equipped with nuclear power and closely linked with American and British propulsion, weapons, and reconnaissance systems. South Korea and Japan are also intensifying their military cooperation with the US, and through the Quad alliance, the democracies of Australia, Japan, and the US, together with India, will hold their naval maneuver off the Australian coast for the first time. Finally, AUKUS plans to extend military-technological cooperation beyond the submarine project to the areas of artificial intelligence and cyber technology.

Against this background, Germany will hardly be able to avoid following up its Indo-Pacific guidelines, adopted in 2020, with concrete initiatives that underline its claim to ambitious security policy engagement beyond the symbolic dispatch of a frigate (August 2021) or the participation of the German Air Force in a maneuver in northern Australia (2022). Certainly, there will not be a permanent presence of the German Navy anytime soon. The extent and permanent commitments in the European neighborhood from the Baltic and North Sea across the Atlantic to the Mediterranean do not allow this. However, the rotating dispatch of German combat ships to the region, the expansion of technology partnerships and arms procurements, and regular exercises with regional partners would be the least that allies could expect in the medium term.

However, the opportunities in the Indo-Pacific region are still as untapped as the potentials in trade with Africa. In both cases, they are limited to regular exchanges and the initiation of joint projects, without any significant changes in the increase and diversification of raw material exports from the region. Indonesia, India, the Philippines, Australia, Japan, or Myanmar are all potential candidates for such partnerships with high global market shares for nickel (Indonesia and Philippines), rare earths (Myanmar), or lithium (Australia). They have the advantage over African partnerships that they, with the exception of Myanmar, have comparatively stable domestic political conditions. In the case of Morocco, from where Europe obtains a large part of the phosphorus indispensable for fertilizer production, the unresolved Western Sahara conflict has repeatedly led to export disruptions in the past. The situation is even more delicate with regard to the Democratic Republic of Congo, which is chronically plagued by internal and military conflicts and from which the EU obtains almost 70% of its cobalt needed for battery production and 35% of its tantalum needs. In all cases, the funding instruments of the federal government can be used to support financially intensive and risky raw material projects in the long term (Kullik 2021). And one should by no means be guided exclusively by the principle of "friend shoring". This reduces diversification and makes the economy more susceptible to shocks.

Finally, there remains one last instrument that Germany should make more use of via the EU and in cooperation with the US, as long as there is still time. Although the EU now uses the sanctions sword much more frequently than in the past, it remains behind its possibilities due to the principle of unanimity, especially in the financial sector. China will do everything in its power in the remaining 2020s to become independent of the dollar-dominated global financial system. And it is likely that the Chinese renminbi will gain market shares at the expense of Western currencies such as the dollar and the euro in the medium term. Saudi Arabia has already suggested to the leadership in Beijing that the oil obtained from Riyadh should be denominated and settled in renminbi in the future. Alipay and WeChat Pay are used by a billion Chinese for transactions also on global markets.

However, China's dependencies and those of the global economy on both leading world reserve currencies and a global banking system still dominated by the dollar are still large. The US and the Eurozone still have a strong geo-economic lever against the rest of the world in the area of so-called non-direct investments in the form of portfolio flows and cross-border loans and deposits. In the case of (secondary) sanctions, recipient countries lose access to global financial markets and thus risk being cut off from trade flows still predominantly invoiced in dollars. The renminbi is still far from being able to exert a comparable leverage effect on European and American economic interests in return.

For this reason, Germany should invest more in the expansion of European financial and monetary policy, for example by delegating financial sanction competences to a "European Office for Foreign Assets Control" comparable to the American Office of Foreign Assets Control (OFAC), or also in the area of a long-discussed digital European central bank currency. Any measures are not only an important signal to China that Germany is willing to strengthen the European economic and monetary area in global geo-economic competition. They are also a sign to Washington not to overstretch the instrument of secondary sanctions with regard to European allies.

Otherwise, dealing with Washington requires more pragmatism. The usual anti-American reflexes in the wake of disappointment over American industrial subsidies under Biden, which were also directed against European companies, are of little help. One will have to get used to them even more so under Trump. Where they harm European partners, these should insist on reciprocity. Beyond that, however, there can be no doubt in Germany about the overriding importance of transatlantic trade in times of global system competition. Russia and China are openly on a confrontational course with America as well as Europe, which should make the still strongest economy in the world more attractive than ever for European companies and should rather encourage politicians to face America's industrial policy challenge (which is by no means new) soberly and not to immediately swing the protectionist club verbally. This is also supported by the still overwhelming importance of transatlantic trade: more than half of global consumption is handled through it, more than 16 million jobs depend on it, and around a third of global GDP in purchasing power parities is generated by it (Hamilton and Quinlan 2024).

Naturally, a subsidy race through a less rigid application of EU state aid law and further debt, as is being discussed primarily in Paris and Brussels, appears attractive at first glance. This could potentially prevent European companies from migrating to the US to a greater extent. However, all political complaints and concerns from the European side have not prevented German companies from investing more money in US projects than ever before in 2023, with a rising trend. This is also due to the simultaneous loss of importance of the Chinese sales market and investment location. At the same time, however, Washington's pressure on European partners not to deliver semiconductor technology and special production technology to China, as they would otherwise face secondary sanctions, reinforces this trend. For German and European companies, the American market is far too important to oppose Washington's demands, especially as the country once again proves to be extremely adaptable in times of crisis and its economy robust.

One can expect that Trump's protectionism will have predominantly negative effects on the German economy. The rigorous "America first" politics will strengthen the US economy in the short term through deregulation and

5 Germany's Previous Economic Model ...

debt-financed tax policy, from which the global economy could also benefit in part. On the other hand, however, the increase in tariffs is likely to cause the inflation rate to rise more sharply by making imports more expensive, which means that the Fed will be able to reduce its interest rates less. The classic reaction on the foreign exchange markets is likely to initially increase the value of the dollar and thus ensure that the American capital market continues to be attractive for investors. However, Trump's fiscal policy and his plans to reduce labor migration could soon have a negative impact on the economy as they increase inflation pressure and further dramatically increase national debt. In any way, Germany should see the new course in Washington as an opportunity. Instead of just speculating about counter-tariffs, you should think about how the situation of your own companies can be strengthened at home and on the world markets - namely through reductions in duties and taxes, lower energy costs, more digitalization and less bureaucracy. And despite all the criticism of the German export model from Washington, it should not be overlooked that then US was still the largest buyer of german products in the last decade and that Germany, with direct investments of almost 660 billion dollars, ranks third among the largest investors in the US. In contrast, trade with China has been declining for years, despite continued greater dependence on the Chinese market compared to Europe. For this reason alone, Trump's foreign trade plans in the medium term are likely to be directed primarily against China although an escalation of the trade conflict with Europe cannot be ruled out either.

Otherwise applies: The still valid IRA package approved by the US government includes nearly $370 billion in financial incentives for investments in "Green Technologies" over ten years. This is less than two percent of the US economic output or about 0.1% of the annual US GDP.

Two-thirds of this is earmarked for tax benefits that are not currently capped, one-third only for grants. In comparison: The "Next Generation EU Program" planned for seven years is significantly larger in terms of annual economic output; on average, EU funding for renewables is €80 billion (Kleinmann et al. 2023). The same applies to the German government's economic shield of €200 billion for just 18 months or France's nearly €100 billion provided for inflation control until early 2023. And all these pots of funding do not yet include the funds earmarked for climate targets from the Corona Recovery Fund (€700 billion by 2026) alone, which amount to 40%. For economies whose GDP is about a quarter of the American one, the accusations of a subsidy race launched by the US seem unbelievable in view of such magnitudes. And the view of the role of the state, Berlin must not deceive itself, has changed significantly during the financial and Corona crisis in Europe.

Instead of panicking about falling behind once again in the technology competition with the US and China, Europeans, especially the two largest economies, should focus on their own strengths and see the opportunities of such subsidies for domestic consumers. While the IRA so far could not significantly accelerate US economic growth beyond the initial increase in spending (Posen 2023a) and was rather an inflation driver for American consumers in the end, because import prices in other sectors where the US lacks free capacities due to the shift towards green technologies were rising, the opposite could happen in Europe. Thus, the American exclusion of companies that do not follow the *"local content"* requirements of the IRA could make Europe a more attractive alternative market, thus increasing the supply of goods here and lowering prices. After all, according to an analysis by the German Institute for Economic Research (DIW), the US obtains about 75% of its critical raw materials from countries with which it does not have a free trade agreement. In addition, it opens up the possibility for Europe and Germany to increasingly source products and renewable energy plants from the US in the future, thus reducing one-sided dependencies on China. The European leeway for the independent China policy of the past will be very narrow in the foreseeable future given the tense relationship between Beijing and Washington. Overall, the trend towards more domestic production thus simultaneously promotes the diversification of international production.

It is also overlooked that the US has lost a lot of attractiveness for foreign investments in recent years, while Germany as a location for innovation even performs better than the US. New foreign company settlements "on the green field" have decreased from nearly $20 billion in 2014 to less than $5 billion in 2021. The massive reduction of the corporate tax from 35% to 21% in 2017 did not change this. This suggests deeper problems that cannot be solved by tax or other financial incentives, as envisaged by the IRA.

Therefore, once again: a subsidy competition harms both sides equally and only benefits some shareholders of the already very profitable tech companies that benefit from such subsidies, and of course the system challengers in Beijing and Moscow. However, from an overall economic perspective, it benefits little and rather leads to greater burdens on other economic sectors. If skilled workers are drawn into less competitive sectors such as chip production with funding from tax revenues, they are missing in other areas. This can also speak against the greater risk of government deficits, especially when such subsidies, as in the case of the IRA, are unlimited. As long as investors in the US comply with the regulations, the state has to pay. Therefore, it depends on whether the government subsidies generate enough growth to service the debt. If the funds fizzle out due to a lack of qualified skilled workers for the new high-tech companies, the potential for inflation increases significantly once again. The intensification of competition for foreign investment by the IRA should therefore lead to increased efforts in Europe to support the retention of local companies through efficiency increases in industrial production; this goes beyond the adjustment screws of unit labor costs, net profit margins and optimized location conditions in the areas of skilled workers and infrastructure.

This does not mean that Europe should not defend itself against distorting American initiatives in terms of reciprocity and proportionality, such as by threatening a digital tax or a CO_2 tariff at the external borders; China and the US do not shy away from such measures either. It also does not mean that Germany should not promote such future-oriented industries together with its European partners that also receive targeted support in Beijing and Washington. It makes sense for companies in Europe to get what they are promised in subsidies and tax breaks elsewhere. And as described above, it also makes sense that in addition to courting companies, restrictions on investments or exports as well as sanctions should be part of the Europeans' toolbox. Despite rhetoric to the contrary, the US has always practiced classic industrial policy in the past by awarding research and development contracts from the Pentagon and buying almost the entire microchip production until the 1960s, which later also enabled the success story of Silicon Valley.

Why shouldn't Europe learn from this? The discussion within Europe has been revolving around the ongoing German-French antagonism between an order policy that strengthens domestic competitiveness, supplemented by social-liberal elements that meet the challenges of globalization (Germany), and an industrial policy that relies on extensive state investments and stronger interventionism (France). The concern about the migration of companies and entire industries in the location competition with the US and China for future climate-neutral technologies is exaggerated regardless of current trends. Germany still lacks the insight that both can work if the interaction between the state and the private sector is designed flexibly enough. Neither the market nor the state regulate everything. European aid for the introduction of new technologies or for research and development is just as sensible as coordination on issues of supply chains, EU regulations oriented towards common goals and harmonized, as well as cross-border industrial alliances. Germany should be more open to France's ideas of European sovereignty in relation to a better coordinated European industrial policy. Just because France's economic prospects have been less rosy in the recent past does not mean that the liability risks resulting from future joint projects must endanger German creditworthiness. And apart from that: Where European projects like the military transporter from Airbus or the carrier rocket of the Arianegroup were put on the back burner for years and thus caused cost increases because Berlin was suffocating in its own bureaucracy and had no reliable access to a technologically capable industry, it should meet French offers with less disinterest than was the case in the past. The armaments cooperation with France failed in Paris not least because the federal government lacked the industrial-technological ability to contribute and was dependent on the industry of other states and their governments, for example when it came to export permits or production guarantees (Mölling 2023).

The tide can quickly turn if the necessary flexibility is lacking: Today, France, long criticized as being hostile to business, has become one of the most popular locations in Europe for foreign investment. Thanks to tax incentives and an overall better economic environment through pension system and labor market reforms, the French investment rate is pointing upwards and industrial promotion is now yielding considerable returns. Germany, on the other hand, is struggling and is in a political crisis that affects its economic prospects, even if it is not yet again the "sick man of Europe". Instead of invoking the old contrast between the two economies and undermining the internal market through national protectionist agendas, people here should be more open to German-French projects that strengthen Europe. This applies to armaments cooperation as well as to the AI and digitization sectors.

It is crucial to look very closely at where such measures pose a risk to competition. The EU's idea that precisely those companies that claim state aid from other third countries may be subsidized by the member states leads to the aforementioned subsidy race and to companies possibly postponing investments in their competitiveness. Moreover, it is in Germany's interest to strengthen its own location and the competitiveness of future industries by improving infrastructure, digitization, and the de-bureaucratization of administration, reliable energy supply, and modern immigration law. This is industrial policy that prevents companies from migrating due to high electricity prices, bureaucratic hurdles, and sluggish approval procedures (as recently in the cases of Tesla's battery factory in Brandenburg's Grünheide or Intel's chip factory in Magdeburg). And here, Germany can still learn from the evidently faster and less bureaucratic path.

References

Hamilton, Daniel, Joseph Quinlan: The Transatlantic Economy 2024, Transatlantic Leadership Network: Johns Hopkins University, Washington 2024.

Hesse, Jan-Otmar: Exportweltmeister – Geschichte einer deutschen Obsession, Suhrkamp 2023.

Huotari, Mikko: Leitlinien für die deutsche China-Politik, in: Internationale Politik (Mai-Juni 2022), pp. 74–79

Hüther, Michael, Jürgen Matthes: Is the U.S. Inflation Reduction Act Hurting the German Economy? An objection to exaggerated claims, Atlantik-Brücke (18. Januar 2023).

Institut für Weltwirtschaft (IfW), Was wäre wenn? Die Auswirkungen einer harten Abkopplung von China auf die deutsche Wirtschaft, Kiel (Dezember 2023)

Jäger, Marcus: Economic Equidistance is not an option, DGAP Policy Brief (20. Januar 2022)

Kamin, Katrin, Rolf Langhammer: Die geoökonomische Leerstalle füllen, in: FAZ 29. Oktober 2021

Kleinmann, David, Niclas Poitiers, André Sapir, Simone Tagliapietra et al: How Europe should answer the US Inflation Reduction Act, Policy Contribution, Bruegel Institute, No. 04 (February 2023).

Kullik, Jakob: Gekommen, um zu bleiben – Deutschlands Engagement im Indo-Pazifik: Strategische Rohstoffpartnerschaften aufbauen, Konrad-Adenauer-Stiftung, Analysen & Argumente (Nr. 464/Dezember 2021)

Mölling, Christian: Rüstungsdschungel Deutschland. DGAP Externe Publikation, Berlin (17. Januar 2023)

Posen, Adam: The weakest link in Biden's Foreign Policy, in: Foreign Policy (March 31, 2023a)

Posen, Adam: The End of China's Economic Miracle, in: Foreign Affairs (August 2, 2023b)

Scharre, Paul: Decoupling Wastes US Leverage on China, in: Foreign Policy (January 13, 2023)

6

The End of Western Complacency

Where is the world heading, where are Europe and Germany heading? The climate for democracies has noticeably cooled at least in the ongoing third decade of the 21st century. Led by Russia and China, autocracies are gearing up to challenge the West—not only to strengthen their power position internally, but also beyond their borders. This is associated with a multipolar (dis)order, in which Europe's desire for "eternal peace" has not been fulfilled. The global turn away from democracy is rather associated with the advance of an authoritarianism directed against the West, which finds its most aggressive expression in Putin's invasion of Ukraine. The decades-long feeling of security is sustainably shaken and demands a change in mentality in Western societies away from the proselytizing towards a pragmatic approach to other power centers of this world.

This is not about giving up the idea of the universality of liberal values, but about recognizing different political, historical, and cultural contexts. Democracies must, however, all the more consistently adhere to the basic rules of the international order, to which the overwhelming majority of the international community of states has committed itself through the Charter of the United Nations. The fight against autocracies will only be successful if the West, on the one hand, lays the foundation for the renewal of its own social contract by taking away the citizens' feeling of loss of security, among other things, due to lack of regulation of global corporations, cyber attacks against politics, society and companies, especially the arms industry, uncontrolled migration or climate change, and on the other hand, forges alliances with those states whose protection from revisionist great power politics lies solely in the consistent advocacy for the basic principles of international law. The West therefore primarily needs partners who do not feel patronized by democratization without participation from the West, but are willing to largely recognize the few central rules of the game in the international system—sovereignty, territorial integrity, non-interference principle and prohibition of violence.

For the future European security architecture after the Ukraine war (regardless of the fact that we cannot foresee its end), the outlines of an order are emerging that resembles that of the Cold War in at least one respect: a more or less united Europe under US leadership in defense against the Russian threat—provided Europe succeeds in convincing Washington that Europe's defense is in its strategic interest. The idea of a rapid EU intervention force, which has its own headquarters and maintains common capabilities, is therefore more vital for Europe than ever. It is necessary so that it is able to stabilize its own southern flank in the future division of labor and to project deterrence towards the east, if possible alongside Washington.

The latter will be the decisive litmus test for the EU and Germany due to the geopolitical shift of Europe's strategic focus towards the eastern member states. Without some form of European army or credible deterrence, Putin will be hard to impress.

As a consequence, Europe and Germany must do everything possible to finally strengthen the European pillar within NATO. If Trump can be convinced of Europe's determination this could also temporarily settle the long-smoldering debate about the future division of labor between NATO and the Common European Security and Defense Policy in favor of the alliance—with consequences also for the post-Brexit relationship between the EU and Great Britain. Through the alliance, London will be assigned a more prominent security policy role in Europe again through the "special relationship" with Washington. If Trump abandons Europe, as appears to be the case as these lines are being written, Europeans, including the UK, have no alternative but to invest in a strong and independent European deterrence.

Anyway, there is no alternative to European "strategic autonomy" in view of the uncertainties about the future direction of the US. However, the idea that the aforementioned change in consciousness in the German population will immediately bring about the necessary change in mentality is unrealistic. Strategic cultures are semi-permanent phenomena, the character of which may change through external shocks, but the forces of persistence should not be underestimated. The high approval rates that the NATO alliance and the partnership with the US have experienced over the last three years show that European societies instinctively sense that this process cannot be brought about overnight and that for this reason NATO and the alliance with the US remain the decisive reassurance for Europe. If Europe wants to keep this reassurance - and there is no guarantee for this under Trump - it must provide all means necessary to support Ukraine and protect Europe without the Americans.

How this can be done is obvious: If major treaty changes in the field of European foreign and security policy are illusory for the time being, but the current world situation urgently requires "more Europe" in this area, there is no way around further flexibility of CFSP. This means, also not a new thought, to strengthen the commonality of those states that are willing to move forward within the framework of so-called "coalitions of the willing" - as currently shown in the case of Europe's effort to support and protect Ukraine without the US. This applies globally, it applies within NATO, where the principle of unanimity also applies, and it must also apply within the EU. Not more communitization, but stronger cooperation of individual member states is the order of the day. For Germany the historic plan to boost defense and the economy by harnessing hundreds of billions of euros for military buildup and infrastructure therefore was the right step, as was the decision to effectively exempt defense spending from the country's constitutional fiscal restraints. The threat to the security of the country and Europe as a whole posed by the Moscow-Beijing axis and now, in a worst-case scenario, even a possible Washington-Moscow axis is real and requires urgent net investments in its defense; this is particularly true for the Bundeswehr, which has been underfunded for decades.

For this reason, the question of enlargement will also remain a major challenge for the Union beyond the end of the Ukraine war, indeed it poses a dilemma for Brussels and the member states. No matter whether the position of the alliance in the end will be strengthened or not, there is a shift of power within the EU in favor of the eastern member states. Washington might continue to support those eastern member states that are willing and have already boosted defense spending through bilateral arrangements outside the NATO framework and at the same time push for an expansion of the EU and an indirect strengthening of NATO for geostrategic reasons—a position it shares with Poland and the Baltic states. This development could increase the costs for the wealthy northwestern member states. In view of the refugee flows from Ukraine towards Poland, calls from the Germans and Dutch for a more liberal refugee policy in Europe will also fall on deaf ears. Nor will Washington support an enlargement policy that insists on sticking to the principle of conditionality. Rather, it will place any enlargement under the primacy of a related strengthening of the alliance and the fight against the systemic challengers without the US having to intervene in any way. However, it remains unclear whether Washington continues to support the goal of Putin's failure and the successor regime in Moscow by all political, economic and military means, as long as a radical change of mind does not take place in Russia. If so, it requires the willingness of Europeans to station American troops and military equipment, but not the pedantic fulfillment of stability criteria.

In view of the costs for the reconstruction of Ukraine, the US will also resort to the old narrative that the EU will primarily have to bear the financial costs for the accession of Ukraine, Georgia, Moldova and the Balkan states (Albania, Bosnia-Herzegovina, North Macedonia, Montenegro, Kosovo and Serbia). The EU would once again become a waiting room for NATO membership, especially since the latter seems unrealistic for the foreseeable future. This in turn is likely to raise the well-known, mainly French concerns that enlargement cannot be had without prior deepening, i.e. a thorough reform of the decision-making processes (Streeck 2022).

The cohesion of the community will thus be stretched to the limit once again. The EU will not be able to evade its responsibility towards the accession candidates. At the same time, however, the circle of "illiberal democracies" is expanding and states are being admitted that feel more connected to the political culture of Putin's Russia than to the European Union. This is also why France has already proposed a "European Political Community" as a precursor to membership, which can also include states where it is doubtful whether they will ever meet the requirements for full membership in the EU.

The question of enlargement thus becomes a tightrope walk for the Union between the legitimate security interests of the accession candidates and Washington's geostrategic interest on the one hand, and the impending inability of the Union to act as a result of possible overstretching on the other. And it is foreseeable that those who speak of a "European sovereignty" or a "sovereign European Union" wish exactly the latter—a Union that is more capable of action than today's.

One thing, however, is clear. Europeans will only increase their global political weight through closer cooperation. This is not only a strategic necessity because Russia and China provide the occasion for it. It is also necessary because the future of their still most important ally doesn't bode well. And even if it turns out differently, the EU, Berlin must be able to guarantee its own security without the US rather sooner than later.

Taken together, this leaves only a pragmatic dual strategy for the EU/Germany during and beyond the Ukraine war: Since the necessary structural and mental change takes years, the security partnership with the US remains indispensable for the time being. At the same time, however, Europe must act as if the American partner had already left. To maintain this European NATO contributions must increase to way more than 50% of current NATO planning. Only if, above all, the European NATO members increase their contribution to strengthening air and missile defense as well as cyber defense on the northeast and southeast flank of the Euro-Atlantic area, and also take Moscow's nuclear options into account, can the deterrent function also unfold its effect in Moscow from a European perspective.

In addition, the assumption of greater responsibility by Europe in the Near and Middle East, joint arms procurement, and above all a more active Asia policy, should help to put the relationship between the Union and the US on a permanently new basis. Whether this would then make the goal of strategic autonomy redundant again, as in the times of the Cold War, may well be the case. However, relying on this would be suicide. Therefore, it is reassuring that both developments always also serve the long-term goal of credible strategic autonomy.

A possibly greater challenge than the security policy threat to Europe and Germany from Russia are the upheavals in the world economy outlined in this book. The worldwide use of economic policy instruments as a weapon against system opponents or competitors inevitably leads to Europe and Germany having to align their trade policy more closely with security interests. Both are in the midst of a technological cold war, which not only has its price, but also puts their open societies under pressure. The analogy of a new Cold War is by no means exaggerated: Just as it was necessary in the post-war period to develop a common front against Soviet expansionism, Europe and Germany today face the challenge of developing a common strategy especially against China, but possibly also the US, by progressive bundling of European forces in the chip and laser industry, AI and quantum research, and genomics or fusion energy, to make supply chains more resilient.

This also applies to the race of ideas, which takes place mainly in social networks; it must concern Europe that almost half of the children between 4 and 18 years old use Tiktok today. What is known as "cognitive confrontation" requires a coordinated approach to more or less natural partners such as Japan, South Korea, India or Australia, but also to developing countries, in order to offer them an alternative model of technological empowerment beyond digital authoritarianism.

For Europe and Germany, this means that they increasingly have to (and must) orient themselves towards the US strategy change towards China. In many member states of Europe, and especially in the EU Commission, China is now perceived as a geostrategic challenge. However, few speak of an open security policy problem. Unlike in France, Germany still finds this assessment difficult and thus blocks a common European China policy. The major German corporations still resist stricter EU measures against Chinese overproduction and thus dictate China policy in Berlin. However, a more restrictive state guarantee for investments is no longer sufficient. A stronger European industrial policy, for example in semiconductor or battery production, is just as necessary for the defense of equal competition rules on global markets and our own competitiveness as a robust defense against coercive measures by third countries. The EU has consistently pursued this path since 2019 and introduced a number of trade policy instruments described above. With the "measures to strengthen economic security" recently proposed by the EU Commission, Europe is advancing on the path to a more "geo-economic" Union. However, export controls, scientific cooperation and increased investment control, including "outgoing investments", do not fully unfold their effect as long as "national security" remains in the hands of the member states.

Industrial policy understood in this way is now also more popular in Germany, but even if Berlin supports the construction of semiconductors and batteries with billions, the expectations associated with this have not been met in the past three years. Corresponding projects were slowed down by inflation, lack of planning security regarding electricity costs or complex and lengthy approval procedures. Regardless of this, one must get used to the idea that de-risking is associated with costs, i.e., trade profits must be sacrificed in the interest of greater security. The establishment of production in sectors where dependence has become too great in the past requires temporary import tariffs and subsidies and by no means guarantees trade profits as long as this only achieves a technological leveling compared to competitors on the global markets. As discussed above, it makes more sense to use geo-economic instruments in the sectors where Europe and Germany have comparative advantages. State aid may be useful in individual cases, but strengthening the location conditions in these areas is more promising.

China's recent advances towards Europe not only show Beijing's fear of a European-American bloc formation against China, but also the mutual economic dependencies between Europe and China. For this reason alone, the key to Germany's future prosperity lies in a dual strategy: First, deterrence and retaliation, as in the case of Russia, are the only effective response at a time when China and other autocracies are increasingly aiming at the isolation and disintegration of the West, and as long as such mutual dependencies of goods and technologies exist; this is particularly true when Europe acts as a unit. Second, Germany and Europe can only achieve economic security by reducing overly one-sided dependencies, even if the price for this is initially renouncing the positive-zero-sum game of global division of labor. Only in this way can pressure be exerted on those countries that have been relying on the use of geoeconomic instruments for political purposes since the global financial and economic crisis at the latest. Regardless of the fact that China's overcapacities have long been a global problem against which not only the US, but also emerging countries like Mexico, Brazil or Turkey are now defending themselves, it is advisable for Europe and Germany to learn from the geoeconomic practices of China and the US and to apply them reciprocally. What Europe has so far done, for example, through tariffs or subsidies, especially in the climate sector, is certainly not enough compared to what the two superpowers enact in regulations to protect their own companies in the interest of national security. With regard to China, it should be noted that it now produces as much as the EU and US combined. Therefore, for Europe and Germany, there can actually only be a coordinated response with the US. At the same time, however, they should not rely on the security and geoeconomic threats to disappear on their own at some point or the US will continue to protect Europe. Only then will the necessary security policy and geoeconomic turnaround be a success.

Reference

Streeck, Wolfgang: The EU after Ukraine, in: American Affairs (May 20, 2022)

GPSR Compliance
The European Union's (EU) General Product Safety Regulation (GPSR) is a set of rules that requires consumer products to be safe and our obligations to ensure this.

If you have any concerns about our products, you can contact us on

ProductSafety@springernature.com

In case Publisher is established outside the EU, the EU authorized representative is:

Springer Nature Customer Service Center GmbH
Europaplatz 3
69115 Heidelberg, Germany